Lessons From The Gibson Girl

Her Quest for Equality, Justice, and Love

• • •

Gary W. Clark

LESSONS FROM THE GIBSON GIRL
Her Quest for Equality, Justice, and Love
Copyright © 2017 Gary W. Clark

Library of Congress Control Number: 2017938304
PhotoTree.com, Wichita, KS

ISBN: 978-0-9907615-7-0

Library of Congress Cataloging-in Publication Data
Clark, Gary
Lessons From The Gibson Girl: Her Quest for Equality, Justice, and Love
p. cm
Includes bibliographical references and index.
1. Women's Rights — United States — History. 2. Women's Studies — United States. 3. Editorial Cartoons. 4. Gibson, Charles Dana, 1867–1944

Published by PhotoTree.com
Wichita, Kansas
www.garywclark.com

All rights reserved. No part of this book may be reproduced or transmitted in any form by any means, electronic, mechanical, photocopying, recording, or otherwise, without the prior written permission of the publisher, except by a reviewer who may reference short excerpts in a review. Phototree.com is a trademark of Gary W. Clark.

Cover and interior design by Gary W. Clark
Edited by Gena Philibert-Ortega

Acknowledgements

I wish to thank my editor and mentor Gena Philibert-Ortega for her valuable input, which always keeps me from wandering too far off chasing bright lights, in addition to her organization and editing guidance. Also, I want to express appreciation to my *focus group* – Allison, Cheryl, Diana, Kim, Lindsey, Marilyn, and Terri – for their honest and beneficial analysis of a working draft, which helped me develop a cohesive theme.

I have benefited from numerous organizations, universities, agencies, and libraries for assistance in research and acquiring images. The genealogy department at the Wichita Public Library in Wichita, Kansas was exceptionally helpful in obtaining archived microfilm from the Library of Congress. The Wichita State University Ablah Library gave me access to a phenomenal collection of original periodicals dating back to 1886, in addition to their comprehensive collection of biographical and historical works. Access to many Library of Congress records and images were invaluable to the content of this book. Also, several Internet sources for archived articles, stories, and information were indispensable. These included Google Books, HathiTrust Digital Library, and Newspapers.com.

Table of Contents

Preface

Introduction – Hooked on Gibson • 9

1. Imagination and Wit • 19

2. Becoming the Artist • 25

3. American Society • 43

4. The Gibson Girl • 65

5. The Gibson Man • 87

6. Rise to Fame • 97

7. A Lesson Gallery • 111

8. A Real Gibson Girl • 205

9. Pursuing a Dream • 219

10. Noir et Blanc • 229

11. Gibson Girl Goes to War • 239

12. Life Moves On • 257

Epilogue • 268

Bibliography • 271

Notes • 272

Index • 276

Books by Author • 278

Preface

Lessons From The Gibson Girl illuminates the thought-provoking satirical artwork of Charles Dana Gibson as he introduced the fictional, and sometimes controversial Gibson Girl to America and indeed the world. She was on the leading edge of the battle that sought to bring equality to not only the sexes, but to many segments of society that were taken advantage of, including the poor and children.

Her reign of popularity and influence coincided with the two decades leading to the passing of the 19th Amendment: *The right of citizens of the United States to vote shall not be denied or abridged by the United States or by any State on account of sex.* As the centennial anniversary of this historic amendment is approaching in 2019, the battles and related social skirmishes that were fought to achieve the milestone should not be forgotten any more than decisive military campaigns fought to keep us free are commemorated.

As a character that flowed from C. D. Gibson's pen, the Gibson Girl became a model of intelligence, drive, and independence that women emulated and men admired. She became a staunch champion of equality, justice, and respect. Graced with balance of *everywoman* in her personality, she became a heroine to a wide array of the turn-of-the 19th century populace: young and old, rich and poor. Remarkably, C. D. Gibson's art, wit, and observations are timeless.

The iconic Gibson Girl cannot be separated from Gibson the artist. He spoke through her. His words and images were influenced by the women in his family and many who surrounded him. Gibson, the man, was speaking from their viewpoint – a perspective he sincerely embraced. His empathy, understanding, and support of women's rights cannot be overstated.

The messages and protests he delivered were rallying cries for those who had been repressed and lessons for those with shortsighted and selfish positions. America was finally casting off stereotyped visions of women, minorities, and even work-place tragedies such as cruel child labor. But not without resistance. Still, C. D. Gibson and his cast of notable actors rose to unmatched popularity in the social media of their time and helped influence America's future.

Created in clever and masterful ink drawings, the Gibson Girl graced classic magazines such as *Collier's*, *Life*, *Ladies' Home Journal*, and *Harper's Weekly*, revealing the good, the bad, and foibles of the rich and poor alike. Progressive and sometimes controversial social values were taking hold in America – championed weekly by the Gibson Girl in one-panel vignettes that anyone could understand.

Sadly, many injustices the Gibson Girl tackled are still prevalent today, and astonishingly gaining fervor in many circles. Compassion is increasingly cast aside by fear-mongers who have taken the art of manipulation to new and frightening heights. These levels of blatant denial or disregard of overt sexism, racism, religious persecution, and other fundamental prejudices have not been seen in many decades. The overused adage of *history repeats itself if ignored* is never so accurate as it is today.

In this book, I wish to share the stories, attitudes, and battles of yesteryear with those who are concerned with today's turmoil. However, to bring balance to the reading, the amusing cartoons and situations that entwine the Gibson Girl help alleviate the sadness of current state of affairs with confidence that the tide can be reversed – again.

– Gary W. Clark

Charles Dana Gibson (1867 – 1944)
Library of Congress

Introduction

Hooked on Gibson

The Gibson Girl, a world-famous fictional character at the turn of the 20th century, was infused with real values from the artist who drew her. Just as many of today's cartoonists project their dreams, observations, and opinions upon their characters, the Gibson Girl was a product of Charles Dana Gibson's life.

She was infused with his charming wit, adventurous spirit, and admirable values. The two were one, yet they complimented each other.

She was his alter-ego, but only in the sense of her outgoing personality versus his bashful nature. Through her, Gibson strived to make the world a better place – while still delivering clever humor at the same time.

C. D. Gibson, as he usually signed his art, poked fun at and chastised controversial or unjust social practices of the time. Primarily through his signature character, he championed women's rights while exploring affairs of the heart. He also fought for the young and disadvantaged, and those who were burdened by religious or ethnic prejudice.

On the lighter side, he created looks and attitudes that many young women and men emulated. If you read anything around the turn of the 20th century, you knew Charles Dana Gibson and his leading lady, the Gibson Girl.

Outside of the names of presidents, kings, and queens, his was one of the most recognized in the world. Beginning in 1888, his artwork appeared in leading magazines nearly every week for thirty years. It was not unusual for his social satire to grace the cover and inside double-spreads of both *Life* and *Collier's* in the same week. In addition, he was in demand to illustrate novels and short stories from best-selling authors.

He was actually uncomfortable that his popularity arose from mostly one aspect of his work, the iconic Gibson Girl. Whether it was an intriguing look, her style and fashion, or the various crusades she found herself in, this New Woman captured the attention of a generation. The Gibson Girl was so popular, he actually became her captive. Not unlike an actor who becomes type-cast, publishers clamored to include her mystique in their magazines and books.

Charles Dana Gibson
Ladies' Home Journal, 1902

He obviously accepted this symbiotic relationship with her since she made him very rich and also gave him an audience for important issues to question, lampoon, or assail. Through Gibson's singular bond with the Gibson Girl, he strived to influence the world with a more just social conscience than it previously possessed.

Keep in mind that in the late 19th century, vast numbers of the population were not well-read. Still, everyone understood a well-drawn cartoon. Readers flocked to magazines that informed and entertained by combining sophisticated cartoons with current events or issues.

Now, one hundred years later, much of the population digests their news from electronic images and entertaining video supplied by countless news and late-night talk shows. The essence of Gibson's messages is still apropos today, only the medium has changed. Assuming he adopted the internet, streaming video, and television, C. D. Gibson would have succeeded just as well in the current era.

A CAREFUL DAUGHTER
"NO, MOTHER, THIS BOOK IS NOT AT ALL FIT FOR YOU TO SEE."
"BUT YOU ARE READING IT!"
"AH, BUT WE WERE BROUGHT UP SO DIFFERENTLY."

A Careful Daughter
Life, March 17, 1904

Fame stemmed from Gibson's artistry and wit. Most of his fans identified not with Gibson himself, but the characters he created led by the Gibson Girl. Frederick W. Morton, editor of *Brush and Pencil*, observed in 1901 that Gibson:

> . . . *describes graphically what he sees, using his own inimitable means of depiction. He has a quick eye for the ridiculous, whether it be manifested in high or low estate, and he hits off absurdities in a telling way.*[1]

He was especially adept at fabricating double entendres or crafting snarky quips, usually directed towards deserving bores. His command of wit and timing set him apart from many contemporary artists who drew nearly as well, yet could not deliver the exceptional punch line.

Was That You I Kissed . . .
Life, December 4, 1904

HE: WAS THAT YOU I KISSED IN THE CONSERVATORY LAST NIGHT?
SHE: "ABOUT WHAT TIME WAS IT?"

To be sure, he possessed marvelous pen and ink skills. Not only did he accurately project the human form and surrounding elements into well-composed drawings, Gibson expressed a subject's emotions with only a few well-placed lines of ink. The sentiment could have been joy, sadness, disappointment, love, lust, or desire as it reached into the reader's conscience more often than not.

This brilliance worked in partnership with his bravery. Not dragon-slaying type of bravery, but the courage to combat archaic norms and traditions that unfairly defined people, especially women.

He fearlessly scolded, chastised, and even made fun of his fellow man's arrogance and condescending ways. In addition, his genius included knowing how far to push a controversial topic. Sometimes he devised a blistering point, yet cleverly walked the tightrope between lecturing his audience and entertaining them. Many men loved it, though they probably laughed at the cartoons while convincing themselves, *that of course is not me*.

He was even-handed and did not hesitate to equally question the follies of men, women, rich, poor, young, or old – and when deserving, praise their wisdom. The everyday populace never failed to give him material by divulging their best and worst sides simply by being who they were in public. He lived in bustling New York City, attended theatre and society balls, took in baseball games and boxing matches, sailed off the New England coast, met royalty in England, experienced bohemian life in Paris, and mixed with hard-working friends and colleagues. From his experiences he endowed the Gibson Girl with sophistication, intelligence, bravery, and a social conscience.

● ● ●

One of her favorite sports.
The Education of Mr. Pipp, 1899

The Gibson Girl was not simply a striking portrait – she experienced life. That was her magic, people related to the characters she portrayed. Joining the Gibson Girl, young women with newfound social freedoms and money were breaking traditional roles as Gibson weaved his leading lady into social, professional, and political scenarios and, of course, love.

The suffragist movement had bravely soldiered on since Civil War times, though by 1890 it still had not won a major nationwide victory. The *New Woman*, as she was popularly labeled, commanded that she be allowed to play golf at her father's country club whether she wore a suffrage campaign button or not. Voting, jury duty, and respect would soon follow.

This era gave cartoonists endless subjects and people to parody. Not to deny the underlying issues were serious and important, there were multiple ways to address them – Gibson used humor.

Many scholars have dissected the Gibson Girl's motives and philosophies while criticizing her actions as if she was a living person, usually in defense of a dissertation. But, the Gibson Girl was complex, as we all are. Gibson gave her emotions, quirks, and fears – all stirred together sometimes. She seemed authentically human, contributing to her popularity. Between 1888 and 1910 she, or her co-stars, appeared over one thousand times in *Life* magazine, in addition to another one thousand combined appearances in *Collier's*, *Ladies' Home Journal* and other magazines.

In spite of her popularity, it is important to note that Gibson did not refer to his women characters as Gibson Girls, the label was coined by the popular press. While Gibson frequently declared embarrassment at the expression, his publishers probably enjoyed the high-profile coverage.

Gibson himself described her as the *All-American* woman, even though his favorite models included a French woman, another of Scottish descent, and his most recognizable model was Irish-American. Of course, with the United States just over one hundred years old, it would have been difficult to actually define an All-American woman except for the Native

American. The country in 1900 was still largely a nation of immigrants.

At the turn of the century, the Gibson Girl was one of the most idolized fictional characters. Preceding the movie and television industry, there were no on-screen stars to worship, though she was followed as if she were real. Today, any number of current famous people capture the attention or adoration of fans. These followers emulate the celebrity in dress, look, and positions. Loves and accomplishments are intensely followed. However, Gibson was clear about giving the Gibson Girl aggressive positions against controversial topics. She was more than a romantic comedy.

Unfortunately, people who are only vaguely familiar with Charles Dana Gibson mistakenly believe that the Gibson Girl was the only character he drew. Yet a broad collection of characters sprang from his portfolio, such as the cross-section of passengers on a ferry boat.

In The Same Boat
Collier's, April 30, 1904

IN THE SAME BOAT.

His heartwarming sketches, such as the portly well-off old man spontaneously pulling a young boy on his sled, endeared Gibson to everyone. The reader may not have agreed with some sketched messages, but surely the most critical of them enjoyed his innocent renditions.

The Spirit of the Day
Life, December 1, 1904

Gibson did not generalize and condemn a whole group for the actions of a few. He was fair, without preconceived prejudices and was likely to praise or reprimand any of those around him – whichever they deserved.

Men might have viewed his artistic creations as a means to keep current on societal and political matters. For decades cartoons channeled messages quickly, sometimes raising the reader's blood pressure.

Gibson usually made his reader smile as they digested a critical point. Since many situations involved women – beautiful ones at that – he kept the attention of even the shallowest man. He seduced them with beauty while presenting his message. Still, he was not shy about exposing men's foibles when warranted and quickly illustrated the errors of their ways.

With his pen and ink, he influenced women in more subtle ways, usually promoting equal rights and joys that were previously enjoyed solely by men. In fairness however, he seemed to believe that equality for the fairer sex meant they needed to strive for improvement also. He would call them out for misplaced weakness. There can be no mistake though, he still possessed a knight-in-shining-armor spirit and would champion their cause with little room left for misunderstanding.

Yet, sometimes a cartoon was just a cartoon. He did not try to move the nation's conscience everyday, some days he just entertained his readers with witty commentary on unique situations.

How Long Should I . . .
Life, August 31, 1899

Young Widow: HOW LONG SHOULD I WEAR MOURNING?
"I'M UNABLE TO SAY. I WASN'T ACQUAINTED WITH YOUR HUSBAND."

Athletic, handsome, and intelligent, Gibson was nonetheless modest and avoided public adulation as he easily moved among society's elite, politicians, authors, and fellow artists. Everyone loved him or at least his work, even those who were on the receiving end of his sharp pen.

Whether known by Dana, as his family and friends called him, C. D. Gibson, or Charles Dana Gibson, he seduced everyone with his cartoons' charms, wit, flattering sketches, and occasional snipes when warranted.

Lessons from the Gibson Girl reveals how Gibson's thoughts are prophetic and relevant to any number of today's challenges and issues. His artwork and words were funny, sad, educational, and brilliant – while gently prodding people to treat each other with respect, compassion, and equality – admirable traits exhibited by the Gibson Girl.

Charles Dana Gibson c. 1890

• • •

Chapter 1

Imagination & Wit

Imagination is the fuel that powers writers and cartoonists along their fanciful journeys. This gift is frequently traced to early childhood and recognized in any number of behaviors such as class clown, family entertainer, or even the quiet artist. A lively imagination runs through them all.

Unlike portrait or landscape artists who recreate actual scenes, a cartoonist or satirical illustrator must take an idea, phrase, or other abstract element and turn it into an eye-catching image. The cartoonist must imagine a scene that does not literally exist – Gibson was a master at drawing visions.

What prompted seven-year-old Charles Dana Gibson to see a pig prancing through the woodlands on its two hind legs while carrying an umbrella? Seems it can only be attributed to an active imagination which was just one component of his genius.

Silhouette, c. 1874
by Charles Dana Gibson
Portrait of an Era, 1936

Where did Gibson's imagination come from? We do not know, but we have evidence of its early appearance. A gloomy evening with his father may have started young Gibson on an artistic journey that provided an outlet for his imagination.

Dana's father, Charles 'Charley' DeWolf Gibson, was a sales representative for a train component manufacturer. The company's office was in New York City, though he spent most of his time traveling around the country selling massive springs that cushioned rail cars from bumpy tracks. A big, kind-hearted man who loved children, Charley missed a good deal of his own children's lives due to work and travel, though when home he devoted much attention to them.

When the boy of five lay ill in bed one winter, his father entertained and taught him how to cut paper silhouettes with scissors.[1] Farm animals, cats, dogs, and other familiar images were the young boy's specialty. The subjects were not simply animal profiles, he portrayed them with movement and unlikely accessories as seen with the umbrella-carrying pig.

Soon, after learning how to cut silhouettes, he formed a partnership with his brother and a neighborhood girl. With his partners supervising and suggesting ideas, he cut out samples of animals, which they displayed on the family's porch steps in hope of profitable sales to passersby.

While on his morning route, the local milkman became their first customer. He requested a cow and horse, a tribute to his profession and the horse pulling his milk-wagon. With skill and quick dispatch, the pair of animals was complete and ready to sell. The milkman cheerfully paid the requested three cents, leaving the children to wonder why they did not ask for more. Their first sale gave them a false sense of success, as it would be their only sale. They soon dissolved the partnership, divided the profits, and went about childhood duties of finding new fun.

His artistic skills were nurtured in part by his mother who purchased art supplies out of the meager household budget. He practiced drawing a variety of subjects from diverse sources, including a weekly French newspaper *L'Illustration*. An artistic publication, it was filled with exotic drawings and paintings – wonderful fuel for the imagination. By his teen years, he was painting backgrounds for high school plays, requiring an interpretation of the scene which helped further develop his imagination.

Chapter 1 – Imagination and Wit

A fine imaginative example occurred in his second year working at *Life*, when he called upon a child-like imagination. P. T. Barnum's circus came to town in March 1887, thrilling people of all ages and walks of life. Gibson, only twenty years old at the time, channeled his inner boy, and came up with a fanciful dream-like image of circus animals and performers marching through town, including the bonus of an elephant scooping up his teacher and scattering books in the street.

The Boys' Millennium
Life, April 21, 1887

THE BOYS' MILLENNIUM
BARNUM IS HERE, THE SCHOOL TEACHER COMES TO GRIEF, AND THE WHOLE WORLD IS A CIRCUS.

Gibson's attention to detail was meticulous; adding little sub-plots such as the elephant stepping on a monkey's tail and intricate background antics. It can be assumed that all the activity in the drawing did not actually occur – it was his imagination at work.

One of Gibson's first cover-art appearances was the June 23, 1887 issue of *Life*. A wistful wife peers out the window towards the moon while her young daughter sits on a nearby chair. The woodcut image was pleasing in itself, yet, it was without meaning – until Gibson penned the caption for *A Wife's Explanation*. Now it became a poignant cartoon, worthy of gracing the cover of a leading magazine.

A Wife's Explanation
Life, June 23, 1887

A WIFE'S EXPLANATION
Violet: MA, HOW DO PEOPLE KNOW THAT IT'S A MAN IN THE MOON?
Mother (sadly): BECAUSE IT'S ALWAYS OUT NIGHTS.

Chapter 1 – Imagination and Wit

Witty dialog became a hallmark of his success. Whether he wrote a sharp-tongued double entendre, a moving declaration, or a simple joke, Gibson was as adept with words as he was with a drawing pen.

This comedic intellect set C. D. Gibson apart from many other illustrators of his time. As evidenced in his earliest artwork, humor was the pronounced characteristic of his drawings.

Young Man, Have You . . .
Life, September 7, 1905

"YOUNG MAN, HAVE YOU BEEN TRYING TO KISS MY DAUGHTER?"
"NO SIR! I'VE BEEN TRYING *NOT* TO."

The Last Ditch
Life, May 22, 1917

Though interpersonal jousting and love interests were his frequent sort of cartoons, his imagination summoned any number of feelings depending on the topic at hand, from critical social editorials to gruesome war messages. Revealing a darker side, this World War I cartoon depicts Lady Democracy, a wartime incarnation of the Gibson Girl, throwing German militarism into a ditch of death. A fervent patriot, Gibson drew some of his best, if not shocking work during the Great War, empowering the Gibson Girl with the strength of a nation.

THE LAST DITCH

Chapter 2

Becoming the Artist

Upon finishing high school, the Gibson family could not afford to send Dana to college. In addition he felt self-inflicted pressure to help support his family as they had supported his schooling and artwork so much. With his art passion increasing and his skills continually improving, he often contemplated how he could actually profit from his labors. Throughout his school years he painted scenes for stage-plays, drew portraits of family members, and diligently practiced his art. Still, these opportunities did not contribute to his or his family's financial well-being.

"THE MOON AND I."

C. D. Gibson's first professional sale, to *Life* magazine.
The Moon and I
Life, March 25, 1886

Somehow, the family scraped together the required fees for him to attend the Art Students' League of New York, a respected school that would see some of the finest American artists walk over its paint-splattered floors. One such student by the name of Fredric Remington would become a world-famous artist, and sculptor – and a life-long friend of Dana's. The struggling artist Robert W. Chambers sat nearby as well, soon forgoing art for a successful career as a novelist. Their friendship became mutually beneficial as Gibson illustrated several of the author's novels over the next thirty years.[1] At this point in life, having no professional art reputation, he nonetheless was forging important and treasured friendships that would last a lifetime.

The evolution of Gibson from a young boy cutting silhouettes to the most recognized and admired illustrator in the world was quite smooth. He was not burdened with lasting failures or deep despair frequently experienced by artists. He never felt compelled to cut off an ear, never sought solace in opium dens, and did not spend the last half of a day downing generous quantities of rum after creating masterful work during the first half of the day. All of those were activities of some of the best known artists and authors in history. Gibson was a well-adjusted All-American boy.

After two years in the Art Students' League, Gibson thought he had improved as much as possible from its tutelage. Matter of fact, he believed he had gained very little knowledge and artistic skill, and felt the need to make a living from the craft, and give back to his family what they had extended to him.

• • •

Publishing thrived in the 1890s. For centuries, pictures were carved into woodblocks and then fastened to a printing press; this was state-of-the-art image printing. The process was labor intensive, expensive and took days or weeks for blockcutters to carve the image. In addition, the artist was not assured his work would be faithfully reproduced, since the blockcutter's skill-level affected the final print.

Benefiting from photographic advancements in the late 19th century, a photo-mechanical process soon replaced the woodcut practice. Using a procedure that was born in photographic chemistry, printing press plates were now created from original artwork in a matter of hours and the final printed page was true to the artist's work.

The importance of this new technology did not just enhance printed images, improved economics allowed magazines and newspapers to develop a new entertainment focus. More pictures could embellish magazine pages for little extra cost. In addition, new magazines debuted that were primarily picture journals, satisfying an insatiable demand by readers. The demand for good artists boomed.

Chapter 2 – Becoming the Artist

Advertising and catalog illustration jobs kept new artists busy and provided a livable, though sometimes meager, existence. In spite of some financial reward, images were typically not signed, limiting the artist's exposure, reputation, and of course bragging rights. This category of work was one step above starving artist. However, these opportunities provided a promising artist with practice and some income. The hardships of a struggling artist did not last long for young Gibson. His work and standing in the art community quickly rose to levels that left poor-paying projects to others less talented.

Early examples of Gibson's catalog and advertising work is difficult to identify as they were not signed and were mostly small projects for local merchants. However, near the end of his commercial career, he occasionally illustrated advertisements for noted companies such as Metropolitan Life, Montgomery Ward, and Ipswich Hosiery. His style of art was now considered retro and appealed to those who held fond memories of earlier work. His name brought instant identification with a product as in the Ipswich Hosiery artwork that deliberately associated the Gibson Girl fame to their line of hosiery.

• • •

Ipswich Hosiery full page magazine advertisement by C. D. Gibson, 1925.

Novels and short stories of the era frequently included illustrations, sometimes just a few, usually no more than ten or twelve. If a novel could be advertised as "Illustrated by" a noted artist, book sales improved significantly.

The illustrator created images that depicted a scene from the book, requiring interpretation of the story much as the author intended, while reinforcing the story's emotion. Gibson was one of the finest artists of the day at visualizing a scene, concept, or storyline and then producing a perfect image.

Gibson's unique skills were a perfect match for adventure and romance themes that dominated early 20th century novels, book topics that are not significantly different from today's bestsellers. Even more exciting, he explored the bold new genre of erotic stories that were increasingly popular.

Many times, magazines such as *Harper's Monthly* and *Scribner's* published these books in serialized installments, in addition to single issue short stories. Gibson's illustrations enlivened the stories and other sections of magazines on a regular basis.

I gathered her to me and …
Prisoner of Zenda, 1898

• • •

Editorial cartoons are one of the oldest, most stimulating, and effective forms of journalism. Benjamin Franklin's 1754 *Join or Die* sketch of a disjointed snake represented the different colonies is one early example; he used it to unite the independent colonies to form a 'more perfect union.' More than one hundred years later, fueled by the divisive Civil War, political or editorial cartoons became even more popular.

Harper's ran a section called the Editor's Drawer for short editorials or commentaries on the times. The 1891 Gibson sketch of a sword-wielding woman standing on the Sphinx's head is a curious but powerful image. It accompanied an editorial that chastised the English cultural invasion of Egypt, brushing aside all things local in favor of converting the land to a British retreat. A metaphor of the conquering Anglo woman was simple but effective.

In the world of illustrations, editorial cartoons tend to be the most forceful if not outright mean when depicting a controversial issue or an individual. The point of these characterizations is to rally the reader to the messenger's point of view while discrediting the opponent – a tactic found in political antics. Many times the artist was simply the one with the pen or brush, while the publisher or editor dictated the subject matter and message.

Some artists enjoyed and specialized in editorial cartoons, even though their talents were much wider. The *New York Times* called Thomas Nast (1840 – 1902) the Father of the American Cartoon.[2] Besides his biting depictions that spanned the Civil War to the turn of century, this prolific artist also created the most commonly recognizable image of Santa Claus, and both the donkey and elephant that still represent the Democratic and Republican political parties, respectively. One of Nast's frequent targets was a New York City mayor who reportedly complained in the 1870s:

> *Stop them damn pictures. I don't care what the papers write about me. My constituents can't read. But, damn it, they can see the pictures.*[3]

This corrupt politician's complaint embodied the very idea that empowered Gibson and others as messengers. The oft-quoted axiom of "a picture is worth a thousand words" is generally attributed to first common use in the early 20th century, with its roots traced back to Japanese or Chinese proverbs. The prophecy of this quote cannot be overstated, as editorial cartoons increased at an astonishing rate in the 19th century.

It should be understood, there is a notable difference between an editorial cartoonist and a social satirist; that distinction would be the entertainment factor of the later. Nast never drew cute little cupids ready to unleash their

The Editor's Drawer
Scribner's, May 1891

Santa Claus by Thomas Nast
Harper's, January 1, 1881

arrows of love into whoever needed it most. His Santa Claus depiction aside, Nast's drawings usually skewered one side of a controversial topic.

Yet, it cannot be denied there are gray areas between editorial and satire. Since the early 2000s, Garry Trudeau's iconic cartoon *Doonesbury* has been frequently banned from the comic page to the editorial page or other location as it offended the local readership or publisher. In general, Gibson's cartoons were not highly charged with such controversy since he found politics quite unsavory.

Still, early in his career, Gibson was at the mercy of editors and was compelled to draw objectionable cartoons. Young and inexperienced artists heeded the boss's directions or found another job, while established artists could influence or even determine the assignment during editorial meetings. After acquiring greater professional stature, when he did take positions on political, economical, and social issues, he drew them with humor. The reader may not have agreed with his position, though they probably still chuckled and enjoyed the sketch.

• • •

Humor magazines in the late 1880s crowded the neighborhood newsstand, filling a well-defined new entertainment genre. Remember, there were no situation comedy television shows or romantic comedy motion pictures. *Abbott and Costello* and *The Jack Benny Show* were not yet radio programs. Wireless broadcasting was in its infancy and primarily used for shipping and military applications. Yet people of the 19th century still enjoyed comedy. Yes, it may be hard to believe our great-grandparents laughed, enjoyed a joke, and could make light-hearted fun of others just as we do.

Magazines such as *Punch, Tid-Bits, Judge,* and *Life* sprang out of the decade, each competing for the reader's sense of humor and nickel. While many formats looked similar, each embraced their own style and personality. Cartoons were scattered among short stories, poems, news items, and commentaries; some were small, some nearly full-page. The cover and double-page centerfold cartoons became coveted placements for the best artists.

The granddaddy of humor publications was the English creation *Punch*, which several American publishers emulated in some manner. This aptly named magazine took swings at all English life, from royals to peasants, mixing in politics, society, love, and everyday happenings. Its artistic master was George du Maurier, a Frenchman turned Englishman who was the bedrock of *Punch* for nearly thirty years. Gibson admired his work immensely, well before they ever met. On the occasion they did meet in 1889, Gibson introduced himself with:

> I'm Charles Dana Gibson. I'm an American. I draw and you have been my master for years.[4]

Du Maurier possessed an artistic and humorous style that became evident in Gibson's work. The Englishman drew beautiful women in flattering and challenging scenarios, while Gibson improved upon the look by contributing emotion to the drawing. While much of du Maurier's work relied on lengthy subtitles to make the joke, Gibson reduced subtitles to a bare minimum and let the characters' expressions complete the joke.

Du Maurier's *A Precautionary Measure* cartoon was the type of polite humor that Gibson soon mastered.

• • •

A PRECAUTIONARY MEASURE

"Now go to school, and be a good boy. And mind you don't use any rude words!"

"Rude Words! Tell me a few, Mummy, and then I shall, know, you know!"

A Precautionary Measure
by George du Maurier
Punch, January 5, 1878

Noticeable from an early age, Gibson gravitated toward the humorous and lighthearted side of life for inspiration, which is traceable back to the dancing pig silhouette and other smile-inducing images.

Gibson sold his first professional cartoon to John A. Mitchell, editor and principal owner of *Life* magazine in early 1886. A simple drawing, now legendary in the illustrating community, is an ink sketch of a dog baying at the moon. Gibson, a boy of only 18 years, was quite proud of the four-dollar check he received. For a teenager still living at home, four dollars was a lot of money in those days.

This seemed easy, so he dashed home to knock out five more sketches, calculating they would be worth twenty dollars to the same publisher. Gibson was drunk with confidence from his first sale, as he forgot the number of times his previous images were rejected. Alas, Mitchell turned away the new images; it was as if he wanted to encourage the boy to do better work, and to not accept quick low-quality attempts. Curiously, the four-dollar dog was nothing spectacular, but Mitchell claimed to have seen promise in the young man's capability.

While four dollars may have seemed an exceptional reward for a single drawing, it spent fast, and there was need for continual income if this was to become a dependable profession. Luckily, the publishing business was growing rapidly and with humor magazines clamoring over each other for readers, there were opportunities for up and coming artists. Gibson submitted drawings to many, if not all, publishing houses in the city. By the fall of 1886, his cartoons were regularly appearing in *Life* and *Tid-Bits* magazines.

Tib-Bits was a 16-page humor tabloid with a sharp if not offensive personality. It published an inordinate number of cartoons that poked fun at less fortunate people, their speech, living conditions, and social lives. In particular, images of African-Americans were reminiscent of cartoons found in the Civil War era. In addition, the political cartoons ordered by *Tid-Bits* were particularly mean-spirited with personal attacks on people, another tactic that made Gibson uneasy. During his early years, Gibson took numerous commissions from *Tid-Bits*, much to his eventual displeasure. *Tid-Bits'* editor was Charles Wolcott Balestier, an employee of publisher John W. Lovell, both accused of pirating other works and general mismanagement. In her memoir, Josephine Gibson shared stories of her brother's work for *Tid-Bits* noting that:

> He [Gibson] had reached a place in his work where he no longer had to jump at the call of Mr. Charles Wolcott Balestier, who instigated the political series and often ordered a drawing at noon "to be drawn, cut made, to the press at 2:45 the same day".[5]

Gibson's relationship with *Tid-Bits* was brief, lasting only one year. His growing success allowed him to move on and avoid unsavory projects. The uneasiness with *Tid-Bits* was not simply a personal conflict with Gibson, it never gained profitability, was sold and renamed shortly thereafter.

After his time at *Tid-Bits* he never made fun of the less fortunate again. Furthermore, this experience may have been a seed that grew into seeking justice for a wide range of topics. He saw the power of his business, and may have just then realized the responsibility of his potential influence.

• • •

DETECTED

Pastor (appearing suddenly): While we all is a watin' fer de funeral serbices toer begin, I doan wan' to heah no moah ob dat glass clinkin' gwyne on in dis yer room!

Chief Mourner: Tain't nuffin but der clock.

Pastor: Dat am de fust clock eber I see what done smell of Apple-Jack!

Detected
Tid-Bits, October 15, 1886
Racial stereotyping, including exaggerated dialogue, was not uncommon in *Tid-Bits*.

Life was about to become more pleasant – at *Life*. While drawing for *Tid-Bits*, Gibson also worked for and developed a close relationship with *Life's* John Mitchell.

John Ames Mitchell was an architect, author, publisher, and artist. He was a throwback to one hundred years or more when renaissance men were educated in a variety of disciplines. One of his many interests included the desire to publish a light-hearted magazine. In 1883, along with co-founder Andrew Miller, Mitchell founded *Life* as a humor magazine. As the majority owner and the creative force, Mitchell was President and Editor, Miller was Secretary-Treasurer.[6]

Following a trend of the time, the first *Life* magazine was all about satire. Starting with the usual sixteen pages, the magazine continued to grow and by 1920 was well over 40 pages. The quality of stories, poems, jokes, and of course the cartoons, appealed to a wider readership than the crude joke magazines, and therefore brought in more advertisers. For two decades, beginning in the early 1890s, *Life* magazine ruled newsstands with its superior content led by Charles Dana Gibson's witty and entertaining cartoons.

From its inception, *Life's* masthead promoted patriotism, reverence, love, and humor – framing weekly artwork for each new issue. The first issue cover included two dancing cupids, God (or at least a winged representative playing a violin), doves flying around the U.S. Capital building, a Paul Revere-like rider on his famous run, and a radiant sun lighting the top of the page. It was a bit over-the-top in feel-good metaphors, but the Mitchell-drawn cover obviously worked well for quite some time. Cupid became the *Life* mascot and was incorporated frequently by Gibson and other artists in their artwork. *Life's* kinder and gentler concept fit Gibson's personality perfectly.

Working for *Life*, he was no longer required to draw degrading cartoons to satisfy a publisher. Furthermore, the quality of his drawings and the crispness of his comedic wit both improved dramatically in his new environment. Appearing just three months after the racially slanted sketch in *Tid-Bits*, the innocent and cute cartoon *A Question of Quality* surely attracted readers to Gibson and his style. What's more, it was an indicator of fun cartoons that he would produce for years to come.

A Question of Quality
Life, January 21, 1887

John Mitchell was an incurable romantic as evident from his writings in addition to his artwork. He wrote whimsical short stories, tales, poems, and comical anecdotes. His 1896 book *That First Affair and Other Sketches* presented five short stories including a fanciful rendition of what really happened in the Garden of Eden, and several Gibson drawings of equal whimsy.

An Enormous Bunch ...

That First Affair and Other Sketches, by J. A. Mitchell, 1896

AN ENORMOUS BUNCH OF FLOWERS IN HIS TRUNK

That First Affair is an amusing tale, not anything the reader would imagine before turning the first page. No religious inferences are offered, just the perils and frustrations of a young man as he talks with all the animals that have mates and families in Eden – before his first affair arrives. It was an innocent parody of a revered story, combining the imagination of Gibson's artwork and Mitchell's literary range:

> *And, later a mastodon, hurrying ponderously, yet joyfully along, with an enormous bunch of flowers in his trunk, nearly trampled the disconsolate bachelor beneath his feet, suggested:*
>
> *"Let me put you on my back, and I'll take you to my wedding. You shall be best man."* [7]

Mitchell was Gibson's friend and mentor for thirty years and essentially a crucial business partner since Gibson's popularity was a contributing factor to *Life's* success. The two were a complementary match. Mitchell was the business, marketing, and managerial genius who kept the magazine on an even keel while becoming the leading publication in its field. Gibson was the creative and artistic genius who not only delivered the perfect image at Mitchell's request. Together, they made a lot of money.

● ● ●

Success does not usually befall an artist in only a few short years – exceptions are notable. Yet, Gibson went from an unknown, unpublished artist fresh out of school to the lead illustrator for one of the most popular magazines quickly. Over fifty of his sketches appeared in *Life* magazine during 1888, a vast majority capturing the coveted double centerfold drawing in addition to the notable honor of gracing five covers.

By this time the daily commute from Long Island was taking a toll on him and jeopardizing the increasing number of jobs that came his way, so Gibson took a studio in New York City. His youngest sister Josephine stayed with him frequently, acting as secretary and social excuse. He regularly turned down invitations to time-consuming social appointments by reminding callers that his twelve-year old sister was staying with him and he could not get away. He was intently focused on becoming a better artist and also yearned to visit England and Paris, which would require considerable work to increase his funds over the usual balances.

Cover illustration

Life, October 10, 1889

A forerunner of the *Gibson Girl* develops a sharp wit.

Mr. Top Heavy: WILL YOU SHARE MY LOT, PENELOPE?
Penelope: YES, IF THERE IS A BROWN STONE FRONT ON IT.

With intense dedication, it appeared Gibson's artistic touch matured with each passing month; yet he still sought improvement. Emboldened by steady income from *Life* and other magazines and the lure of learning from respected masters, Gibson finally sailed to England to meet George du Maurier and then traveled to Paris.

At the time, it seemed an artistic requirement or rite of passage for a serious artist to study in Paris. Dozens of studios populated the Latin Quarter, where the bohemian lifestyle influenced writers, artists, and nascent philosophers nearly as much as studio and classroom time. John Mitchell himself had spent seven years in the City of Lights in pursuit of an architectural education. Perhaps, discussions between Mitchell and Gibson influenced the younger man's desire to study abroad.

This was a magical time for Paris. The Eiffel Tower was just completed as the entryway to the 1889 World's Fair and the city was in a festive mood. Gibson was there to learn; the city-wide party was a bonus.

He enrolled in the respected Atelier Julien, an art studio of exceptional reputation.[8] Having no firm plans as to length of stay, the goal was to learn and improve as much as possible until his funds were exhausted. Unfortunately, several of the advertised masters that were supposed to teach at Julien's did not appear during his brief course of study. This included the acclaimed artist Jules Joseph Lefebvre who was famous for stunning pictures of beautiful women in full nude or otherwise alluring scenes. Meeting this master could have changed Gibson's life, though perhaps we are fortunate Gibson missed Lefebvre's direct influence and developed his own unique style.

As the five hundred dollars devoted to the trip approached exhaustion, he purchased a steamer ticket back to New York. Returning home he now could proclaim 'studied in Paris' on his resume as new commissions flowed his way and the frequency of work for *Life* continued to increase.

● ● ●

The 1890s saw a booming economy, rising standards of living, and frolicking fun. It was also a pivotal time for Gibson, his work became more sophisticated and readers could not get enough of his witty cartoons. Even the most casual newsstand visitor recognized his work from a distance.

Despite blossoming success, life decided to throw a kink in his fairly smooth journey through life. February 1890 unexpectedly brought death to his father at the young age of forty-five. Charley caught a cold while traveling a few weeks earlier, though initially it was not a serious concern.

Upon reaching home, his employer dispatched him to an important customer meeting in Milwaukee despite his lingering illness. Shortly into the trip Charley wrote his wife Bessie that he was:

> . . . *forced to send for a doctor and that his ailment was a new and very stylish illness call La Grippe.*

Charley had contracted the flu, influenza, grippe; it was called a variety of names and was not understood very well. He returned home very sick, though with confidence of recovery since he was a robust man of relatively good health.

Modern medicine had not evolved to where it could effectively treat such illnesses, and the mortality rate was high. Flu epidemics frequently swept the country, just as they do more than one hundred years later. Further complicating Charley's health, his flu progressed to pneumonia.

Everyone in the family was called upon to visit Charley except his eldest son Langdon, who was half a continent away exploring the Colorado River. Nonetheless, hope was still high and the fever soon broke, but too late. His heart endured such a strain over the previous month that it finally gave out on February 19, 1890.

After the outpouring of condolences and services for Charley were complete, the artist-son realized he now bore an even greater responsibility for the family. Three younger sisters, ages fourteen, twelve, and seven, years lived at home with his mother. While the Gibson house was paid off with insurance money, Charley had not saved for the future and left little cushion for his family's living expenses. Dana would need to support his mother and sisters.

• • •

Achieving success was even more important for C. D. Gibson now. His newly inherited responsibilities may have inspired him to work harder, more diligent, and take advantage of business opportunities that he could not have imagined just a short time earlier. Increased demand for his work soon allowed him to have satisfaction that his mother would be comfortable and his sisters become educated.

He captured his first cover for *Life* in early 1887 with a young boy objecting to a doctor's bribe to take his medicine. This would be just the first of many covers as his worked appeared in over fifty issues of *the magazine* in the next year.

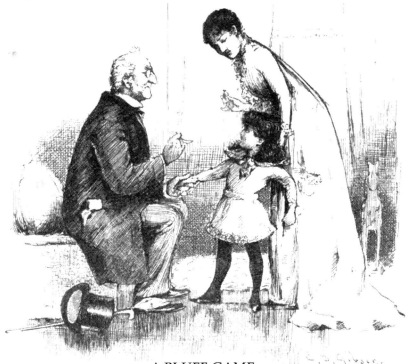

A Bluff Game
Life, April 14, 1887

A BLUFF GAME.
Doctor: NOW, MY LITTLE MAN, YOU TAKE THIS MEDICNE AND I WILL GIVE YOU FIVE CENTS.
Young America: YOU TAKE IT YOURSELF AND I WILL GO YOU FIVE CENTS BETTER.

Lessons From The Gibson Girl

Charles Dana Gibson, Artist.

New York, March 19. — Twenty-two, smooth faced and famous. That meagerly describes Charles Dana Gibson, the artist who's work has become familiar to every reader of high class illustrated American periodicals. His weekly cartoons in *Life* . . . and the dozens of other pictures from his pen which have been given to the public during the last two or three years have established his reputation and made his work eagerly looked for.

Gibson is a tall jolly young fellow with a strong face and pleasing voice. His working quarters on Broadway consist of two rooms, with walls literally hidden by pictures donated by brother artists, interspersed with some of his own.

He is a rapid worker and catches more of the real spirit of modern society in his pictures than any of the many artists who have tried it. There is always an air of gentility and ease about Gibson's men and women. Doubtless one reason for this is the fact that they are all drawn from life. . .

The Olean Democrat
March 26, 1891

Gibson's reputation flourished with the help of such admiring reviews as this newspaper article in March of 1891. His drawing style, grace, and affect on readers quickly became the standard by which others in the field were measured.

His signature wit was harmless yet entertaining like the December 12, 1889 *Life* cover where he chided the rebellious trend of treating marriage engagements as if they were simply trial commitments. The cartoon addressed a questionable trend in a humorous manner – with either a naive response or an example of the Gibson Girl's sharp mental prowess.

IN AMERICA.
"I HEAR YOU ARE GOING TO BE MARRIED."
"NO; I'M ONLY ENGAGED."

In America
Life, December 12, 1889

Chapter 3

American Society

The late 19th century gave us the Gilded Age, a time of unprecedented economic growth, increased wealth, and the concentration of power in the hands of a few. Money from railroad fortunes, oil barons, and steel industrialists empowered the nation as electric machines and assembly lines were increasing productivity. Urban trains, streetcars, and soon automobiles, moved people quickly to work, theaters, museums, the seashore, or other destinations.

A Constitutional in the Park
London, 1897

The Streets of New York
Life, April 22, 1897

Mark Twain coined the term "Gilded Age" in his book of the same name, meaning "the period was glittering on the surface but corrupt underneath." The era fostered government corruption and ruthless trusts, and monopolies, and worse, not everyone enjoyed the benefits of a rising standard of living. As an unintended consequence, this booming prosperity of the few helped trigger social changes across America.

THE STREETS OF NEW YORK

So began a pivotal time in U.S. history as the Gilded Age gave way to the Progressive Era around the turn of the 20th century. Part of this movement focused on curtailing abusive practices by special interest groups, which ironically are recognized today as lobbyist, conglomerates, and takeovers.

Gibson was not the first to lampoon society, business, and politics. Yet, he was fortunate to tackle issues at the same time that printed media was being devoured by readers with an insatiable appetite for fresh content.

Young readers, who typically support if not instigate change, embraced new journals and magazines with edgy stories and images. This movement cannot be dismissed as any less important than the affect of today's instant social communications that can bring down a person or build a nationwide movement in hours. Comparatively speaking, the 1900 millennials were not much different from their namesakes in the 21st century.

• • •

The suffrage movement plodded along through 1900, winning full suffrage in a few states, yet losing at the national level. Many suffrage associations and local chapters lobbied for legislative changes throughout the country, but their fragmented efforts were insufficient to pass a U.S. constitutional amendment. However, at the height of Gibson Girl mania, increased self-realization of personal worth and rights, and implementation of new suffrage tactics helped spur momentum towards real changes within a few years.

Two important suffrage organizations merged in 1890 bringing together prominent leaders into a single organization, the National American Woman Suffrage Association. A notable strategy of the new organization was to recruit "wealthy members of the rapidly growing women's club movement."[1] The idea was that influential women with free time and financial independence would inject new energy into the equality movement. Coincidently, many of these women were keen followers of Gibson's work.

Gibson and his army of characters arrived at a perfect time in history, a point where he could help move things forward by inspiring those who were not hopelessly mired in archaic beliefs.

Lessons From The Gibson Girl

The Jury of the Future
Life, April 11, 1903

One of the long held practices in the United States was forbidding women jurors in the court system. Though jury duty was not part of the 19th Amendment granting women voting rights, it was loosely linked to the suffrage movement. Although many states allowed women jurors by 1900, New York and others still prohibited them from serving until just before World War II. Gibson's *Jury of the Future* clearly captured a cross section of potential jurors, keeping the issue in the forefront of civil discussions.

THE JURY OF THE FUTURE – ONE THAT MIGHT TEMPER JUSTICE WITH MERCY.

Sporting activities provided Gibson with ideas and opportunities to address inequality, which frequently upset traditional boys' clubs in the process.

The confident young woman's alert of *Fore* was not merely warning of a forthcoming golf ball, it was a herald of changes to come. Though it did threaten the heads, or more accurately, the minds of many.

Fore
Life, March 15, 1900

The golfing term 'fore' is of Scottish origin, traced back to at least the 1880s. Interestingly, before its adoption by golf, legend has it embodying a more dangerous implication. An anecdotal description of the short, but hazardous expression includes:

> *The term means 'look ahead,' and it is believed to come from the military "beware before," which an artilleryman about to fire would yell alerting nearby infantrymen to drop to the ground to avoid the shells overhead.*[2]

Instead of dropping to the ground for protection, stodgy gentlemen in exclusive golf environs all over the world probably retreated to dark wood-paneled fortresses within their clubs, cocktail bars known as the 19th Hole. Here they would grouse about an impending female invasion and plot a defense with abundant drink and through a thick haze of cigar smoke.

Still, Gibson positioned women characters in a variety of sports and leisure activities that raised the hackles of the establishment who felt the pastimes were unhealthy, immoral, or improper for the gentler sex.

Sports represented the greatest privilege of male bastions. Sporting games stem from men literally battling for survival over hundreds of thousands if not millions of years. Cravings from the ingrained traits of hitting, throwing, or launching something that was required to bring food to the hearth were replaced by sports. Sharing these physical activities with women threatened the exclusive male club. Men dreaded the thought of sharing their sports world with women as surely it would lead to them wanting a piece of the intellectual arena also.

A line needed to be drawn in the sand – the baseball diamond, sand trap, wherever required. It was scratched out of words, rules, and laws when possible, all constructed by those in power to keep women in their place. One of the first sports-equality battles at the end of the Gilded Age seems absurdly silly today.

Of all the female incursions into sports or leisure activity, no pursuit caused more alarm in cloistered hallways than that of women enjoying the simple pleasures of riding a bicycle.

As the 1890s approached, a bicycle craze was sweeping Europe and America, encouraged by the introduction of the safety bicycle. Early bicycle models, known as high-wheelers, incorporated a very large front wheel with pedals directly attached to the hub. A small wheel trailed behind, with the rider sitting above the front wheel preventing their feet from reaching the ground. This type of bicycle was the province of men – usually athletic men. They were dangerous, as 'headers' were frequent when the large wheel hit a formidable bump in the road and the rider was catapulted head-first over the front. The only way to pause or stop a high-wheeler was to leap off or slow down and precariously lean against a street light pole, building, or whatever was convenient. They were ridable by only the most daring or foolhardy.

The safety bicycle design is the model we are familiar with today. Two equal-sized wheels are powered by a geared chain, with the seat between them, and short enough so the rider can straddle the machine and place his feet on the ground. Also, one of the nicest advancements of the safety bicycle was improved rider comfort as a result of pneumatic, or air-filled, tires that replaced steel rims. It only took the Gibson Girl to make it fashionable, but not without a fight.

The first issue raised was, how a woman could keep her dress in its proper place. Women in pants were still twenty-plus years from being tolerated, full acceptance was not common until the Second World War.

One solution was to wear bloomers, but they elicited nearly as much uproar as did the bicycle itself. They represented women stepping "into everything else hitherto reserved for men" according to Reverend T.B. Hawthorne, D.D. This message became a common chorus expressed by many opponents to nearly every aspect of equal rights for women. The good reverend continued with his clearest proclamation that "women were riding to the devil in bloomers."[3]

Nearly ten years later, even the progressive *Life* magazine published a guest editorial in the August 23, 1904 issue that echoed the fear of women usurping men's rightful monopolies:

> *Those sleepless reformers, Lady Henry Somerset and Miss Frances Willard [English and American suffragists respectively], whose heads are forever getting together over some plot for curtailing the privileges of men, or amplifying the dimensions of woman's sphere have resorted it seems to a strategy to get women into trousers.*

Curses! Women in trousers would curtail the privileges of men. Yet, clothing problems were the easiest gauntlet to run.

More scandalous, a myriad of physiological and sexual imagery were brought up, to the horror of everyone. Graphic descriptions of health hazards and sexual arousal accusations caused by bicycle riding were common cries from experts and moralists. These hurdles needed clearing before females riding bicycles was an accepted activity.

Scribner's, June 1895

The July 1898 *Dominion Medical Journal of Toronto* offered:

> E. D. Page also teaches that the bicycle causes masturbation in women and girls . . . No woman should ride a bicycle without first consulting her medical man, and should ride only when suitably dressed.[4]

There were countless papers and articles with similar alarms, supposedly with the foolish purpose of reversing the excitement of a new mode of travel, exercise, and entertainment. One of Gibson's 1897 cartoons teased the medical fear-mongering by asking the double entendre question "Is Bicycling Bad for the Heart?"

Is Bicycling Bad for the Heart?
Life, June 10, 1897

IS BICYCLING BAD FOR THE HEART?

Besides Rev. Hawthorne's criticism of bloomers, the clergy were quick to play the "woman's place is in the home" card, fearing a suffrage connection and predicting certain damage to women. The January 1902 *Ladies' Home Journal* led with a three-quarter page viewpoint by J. Cardinal Gibbons, Archbishop of Baltimore, titled "The Restless Woman" in which he relentlessly used biblical verses and his own arguments against women in sports and other less-womanly pursuits which violated their "well-defined places:"

> *That woman was created to fill certain well-defined places in this world no one family with her physical, moral and mental makeup can doubt.*

The Restless Woman
Ladies' Home Journal,
January 1902

After berating women's equality in matters outside their well-defined duties and the home, he also highlighted a dedication to sports as evil:

> *I see no harm in a woman's taking part once in a while in a game of golf, or any other outdoor exercise that befits her station. She is not to be housed like a plant, and never allowed the benefits derived from fresh air and moderate exercise. Any proper outdoor pursuit should be encouraged as an occasional recreation, but as a regular avocation it must be condemned.*[5]

It seems as if the cardinal's message included the idea that women could flirt with casual exercise and fun, but heaven forbid she try to become equally proficient with men.

Bishop Gullem...
Life, October 4, 1894

BISHOP GULLEM AT THE ADVICE OF HIS PHYSICIAN TAKES OUT-OF-DOOR EXERCISE.

Shortly afterwards, *The Ladies' Home Journal* seemed to counter the cardinal's position by publishing a two-page article titled "How Charles Dana Gibson Started." The story, written by his friend and *Scribner's* publisher Robert Howard Russell, included no less than seven self-assured women of the typical Gibson Girl style, including a 'sporty' one, a 'flirty' one, and an 'ambitious' type; all which the cardinal would surely condemn. Gibson was usually ahead of controversies, eight years earlier he depicted a fictional Bishop Gullem bicycling with two stylish young women, following his doctor's orders to increase exercise.

Susan B. Anthony summed up her thoughts on the subject of bicycles in 1896:

> *Let me tell you what I think of bicycling. I think it has done more to emancipate women than anything else in the world. It gives women a feeling of freedom and self-reliance.*[6]

Charges of moral decay were abundant. One must remember that full suffrage for women was still more than two decades away. Not only were women treated as if incapable of understanding the process of elections and issues, now they would be deprived of the liberty of physical activity and fun freely enjoyed by men and children. Charles Dana Gibson and his athletic Gibson Girl would champion their cause.

• • •

Golf clubs in the 21st century for the most part have opened their doors to women, though actual data is sketchy as most member-selections are by secret committees. One of the most glaring examples of the century-old custom of restricting women is Augusta National Golf Club's reputation.

This exclusive club has extended three token memberships to women, mostly under duress. Former Secretary of State Condoleezza Rice and investor Darla Moore were both invited in 2012. Under increasing scrutiny, especially since the club hosts the prestigious Masters Tournament, IBM CEO Ginni Rometty was invited in 2014. Coincidently, IBM is one of the long-time sponsors of the Masters Tournament, and all preceding IBM CEOs were invited when they assumed office. Rometty was not invited until after two years in office. One has to wonder if corporate backlash, critical press coverage, or outrage on social media influenced Augusta National's decision to extend membership, stingy as it was, to women.

Worse offenders exist, the most grievous being the Burning Tree Club in Bethesda, Maryland (not to be confused with the Burning Tree Golf Club of Greenwich, Connecticut). So secretive is the Bethesda club, they do not maintain a website. Though the club occupies a noticeable physical space fifteen miles from the U.S. Capital, its secretive influence is imperceptible to the average person.

An Exclusive Men's Club
Harper's, January 31, 1891

The golf information web site oobogolf.com notes the course is:

> ... *a men-only club, women are allowed only for four hours on a single Saturday before Christmas to shop for their husbands in the pro shop. Otherwise, women are not welcome on the course or in the clubhouse and are typically escorted off the property.*[7]

Membership to the uber-exclusive Burning Tree club is by invitation only and typically extended only to former U.S. Presidents, politicians, lobbyists, and men in related fields – male only. Reportedly, this den of power brokers does not even include women's restrooms.[8]

Chapter 3 – American Society

These types of organizations are certainly legal, assuming they receive no government funds. Ironically, the majority of funds that flow into this club come from politicians paid by the U.S. government, contractors funded by the U.S. government, or lobbyists whose funds are raised to influence U.S. government policies through elected officials.

She: I SOMETIMES WONDER WHETHER ALL THOSE THINGS YOU SAID TO ME WERE TRUE.
"WHAT DIFFERENCE DOES IT MAKE? WE BOTH BELIEVED THEM."

I Sometimes Wonder...
LIfe, September 19, 1901

The guarded and exclusive nature of many golf organizations are the most blatant of past and current sexist practices. However, these offending examples are not high profile in the average person's awareness, partly due to the secrecy that cloaks the club's activities. Other misbehaviors touch the everyday lives of everyone.

• • •

The Coming Game
Life, November 21, 1895

Schoolgirls in contemporary sport programs have not escaped the practices of 19th century prejudices as preferential treatment, usually budget-driven, favor men's sports over women's. This inequality is evident in primary and college school systems. Addressing the issue in a not-so-subtle manner, Gibson drew an exaggerated scenario in his cartoon of Vassar College, an all-women school at the time, playing football against all-male Yale University.

THE COMING GAME
YALE VERSUS VASSAR

His point was well made as his sketch represented more than a mere football play. The panicked look on the boy's face and the young woman's determined glare said that women could do as well as men at any endeavor. (It is ironic that neither Yale or Vassar became coeducational until 1969.)

Sadly today, laws are needed that force school districts, college presidents, and regents to refrain from discriminating against young women. The controversy over Title IX (a federal law that prohibits discrimination on the basis of sex in any federally funded education program or activity) should not be that it exists, but that it was needed in the first place. Large and expensive programs such as football in top tier Division I schools should be proud to help fund less lucrative programs that benefit all students. This paradox is a remnant of 19th century values and practices that Gibson recognized as out of place even then.

Sports Illustrated's special contributor Steve Rushin recently wrote about sports' influence in many sectors of life, noting a bobble-head doll and baseball-like card were created of Pope Francis during his 2015 visit to the United States. Sandwiched between entertaining sports and papal analogies in Mr. Rushin's story, he succinctly summed up the role of our sporting games by noting:

> *Sports are a metaphor for every facet of life.*[9]

If Mr. Rushin is even remotely correct, sports inequality is a reflection of discrimination in any number of cultural arenas.

Life Cover
Life, June 7, 1900
Themes were used for many magazine issues. *Life's* Sporting Number covered a variety of men's and women's sports. A Gibson-drawn equestrian graced the cover in her best riding clothes and crop.

• • •

Consumed by a compulsive demand for status, the American nouveau rich became fascinated with old-world royalty and how to become a part of it. The infatuation with English and continental aristocrats, whose financial conditions were at a low point, prompted the wealthy elite to buy their way into exalted titles. Contrived marriages between young American women from successful families and a man with Duke, Prince, Baron, or Count in front of his name was a practice commonly seen in the society pages.

Gibson took a personal affront to this practice, perhaps his impassioned American patriotic spirit considered it selling one of the country's most prized assets, the American girl. He blamed both parties, foreign and domestic.

The 19th century was not kind to European royalty as wars drained kingdom and principality vaults. In addition, most countries were now governed by some form of democratic rule, and royals were many times left to financially fend for themselves. Since plundering neighboring countries to refill royal treasuries was becoming less of an option, new sources of money were needed to maintain the castles and keep the aristocrats in a lifestyle to which they had become accustomed.

King in Reduced Circumstances...
Life, June 27, 1895

"IF WE GO TO EUROPE CYNTHIA, I DON'T WANT YOU TO MARRY ANY OF THEM COUNTS OR DUKES. YOU JUST WAIT UNTIL WE RUN ACROSS SOME KING IN REDUCED CURCUMSTANCES."

With fortunes in the United States swelling, a matrimonial form of *Let's Make a Deal* became popular. The American new industrial rich possessed the money and young potential brides while the royals owned titles. Titles were bought with flesh and cash.

Gibson assailed contracts where a bride brought large sums of money to the marriage. The more money a family was willing to contribute, the more illustrious title they could buy.

Ironically, Gibson's youngest and perhaps his favorite sister flirted with an European aristocratic marriage, not once but twice. Josephine met Sir Thomas Lipton of Lipton Tea fame in 1903 while he was a challenger in the America's Cup Yacht Race. Though thirty years her senior, some fascination must have developed in both directions. She sailed to Ireland the following January for a planned five-month trip to the baronet's country estate in Ireland and accompanied him on trips to Gibraltar, Naples, and other ports.[10] Evidently nothing of a permanent nature developed between the two. She moved on.

A closer call with royalty for Josephine occurred in 1912 with her engagement to a Sicilian count, Francisco Alinasis. However, citing 'drifting apart', Josephine's sister announced in May the engagement was "broken positively and we do not look for a reconciliation."[11] After growing up in and around New York City, the idea of living in a Sicillian villa, where she was expected to reside, may not have appealed to her.

His sister's escapades did not dampen Gibson's critical cartoons of foreign marriages neither before, during, or after her liaisons. This could have made for some interesting family gatherings. Gibson always drew things that surrounded his life. He probably drew upon personal experiences as well, even if the result was to needle his sister. The following cartoon was published just days before the official breakup announcement of her engagement to the Count, leaving the reader to interpret it how they wished.

Lessons From The Gibson Girl

AMONG THE FOREIGN NEWS
THE ACCOUNT OF HER WEDDING ABROAD

Among the Foreign News
Life, May 8, 1912

In a similar vein, yet for reversed reasons, many young women turned to older men for their spouse, motivated by the man's financial standing and sometimes at the behest of a greedy mother. Gibson took as many stabs at this practice as he did towards purchased titles.

Gibson thrust his pen and ink wrath on brides, their mothers, royals, and even the clergy for being part of the purchased charade. Of the social issues he addressed, Gibson may have drawn more cartoons on this single subject than any other. And, unlike most of his work, his commentaries on the matter were not kind.

THE AMBITIOUS MOTHER AND THE OBLIGING CLERGYMAN.

Ambitious Mother
Life, June 5, 1902

• • •

Economic social gaps, particularly in the money centers of New York, Boston, Philadelphia, and Washington D.C. were noticeably wide and more pronounced than during any time in U.S. history except for the slavery and post-slavery eras of the South. New industrial riches did not flow down the social ladder proportionately, while union battles, homeless families, and child labor practices were shuffled out of site from Fifth Avenue wealth.

Concern for orphans and the malnourished became a focus of interest around the turn of the century, especially since it was so prevalent in large crowded cities. *Life* founder John Mitchell, along with *Time Magazine's* Horace Greeley, founded the Fresh Air Fund in 1877 to provide summer camps for underprivileged children. Mitchell regularly wrote about the organization and published contributor's names and donation amounts in *Life*, while Gibson contributed both money and inspiring cartoons to the noble cause. Mitchell's timeless efforts continue into the 21st century as the Fresh Air Fund (www.freshair.org) continues to help "unlock their limitless potential"[12].

Fresh Air Fund
Life, July 30, 1891

WHAT OUR FRESH AIR FUND IS DOING.

Gibson's upbringing and values were at odds with many of the trends taking place in the new industrial age. Manipulative and sometimes cruel child labor practices were a frequent target of serious critiques. He captured the soulful sadness of a young girl trudging off to work in an effort to chastise those who would take advantage of her.

THE ARMY OF WORK
TO EMPLOYERS OF CHILD LABOR

Army of Work
Colliers, July 23, 1904

Unfortunately, most of Gibson's work promoting children's causes and criticizing unfair practices are usually ignored in reviews of his art. Lost over the last hundred years is the recognition of his efforts to affect the social conscience of his readers as well as entertain them.

• • •

An analysis of Gibson's talent and style in 1891 by *Brush and Pencil,* a publication of the Metropolitan Museum of Art, offers an early insight into Gibson's essence:

> *He does not hold shams and weaknesses up to scorn, he simply exposes them pictorially to amuse, to provoke a smile. Some one has said that the artist who can amuse without searing heartstrings or corrupting morals is a public benefactor . . .* [13]

Gibson was not interested in offending or castigating others, his approach was to illuminate the error of their ways using humor. Mr. Robert Bridges, in a 1904 *Collier's* article entitled "An Appreciation," reinforced the missionary style of Gibson's influence:

> *. . . it should be emphatically said that Mr. Gibson has never used his satire to make fun of what is worthy and ideal, but that it has been directed against sham, hypocrisy, and self-deceit.* [14]

Whether Charles Dana Gibson and the Gibson Girl changed the surrounding air with his cartoons may be debatable – it is defensible to think he did. However, after one hundred years of unimaginable prosperity, the greatest country in the world has yet to solve many of the same wrongs that Gibson and his characters tried to right.

• • •

Chapter 4

The Gibson Girl

Many questions have shadowed the Gibson Girl legacy for over a hundred years. Was she real? A composite of several women? Or a creation of Gibson's imagination?

The answer is all of the above, even though a huge number of specific attributions and claims were made as to the original Gibson Girl's identity. In his wonderful book *Portrait Of An Era, As Drawn by C. D. Gibson*, Fairfax Downey mused:

> *It came to be said that the passenger list of the Mayflower, as it lengthened through the years, was a brief document compared to the roll of original Gibson Girls.*[1]

During a trip to London, Gibson observed a billboard claiming the "The Original Gibson Girl Appearing on Stage," yet he knew nothing of the performer. Similar claims to being a Gibson Girl were probably spread by countless young women in New York and elsewhere.

Many different models were employed by Gibson, adding speculation of her origination. The models were real, though some drawings were executed with artistic license. One of his favorite models even insisted that he draw only her face, and used others for the body. Those with a wide range of looks and emotions appeared in multiple sketches, sometimes over several years. Models less talented may have appeared but once.

U. S. Postage Stamp, 1998

Part of the Celebrate the Century Series

– 65 –

Outside the studio he traveled the streets of London, Paris, and New York with a sketch pad, and later finished the scenes by filling in details with his imagination.

• • •

Long before he became an acclaimed artist, women exerted a strong influence on Dana Gibson's drawings, shaping his view and respect for them. His mother, Josephine Elizabeth 'Bessie' Lovett Gibson, nurtured his artistic talent and goals while being the primary parent much of the time as his father was a traveling salesman. His grandmother, Josephine DeWolf Lovett, gave him a "useful gift of a sense of humor" and furnished him with some of the first jokes he illustrated for *Life*.[2] Three younger sisters looked up to him as a storybook big brother in a happy household. Dana recalled,

> *Our home was free from personal strife, and harsh words between our parents were unthinkable.*[3]

Normal boyhood crushes are recounted by his sister in her family book *Longfield: The House on the Neck*. In a quiet moment between Dana's parents, his mother revealed to her husband,

> *Did you know . . . that Dana walked home all the way to Bristol with Cordelia Allen?*[4]

His mother was evidently pleased with her fifteen-year-old son's interest in a young girl, and was delighted with the distance he went to impress her.

His personal relationships with women were not something he shared openly with the world, but glimpses of his life around the opposite sex are available. From the moment his drawings became a hot item among publishers, there is little doubt his reputation and good looks were attractive to any number of women he met.

• • •

Professional models sat for most of his work, while friends who gladly sat for free also become part of his gallery. At various times a model would come into his studio and immediately begin to undress, thinking she was sitting for an *au naturel* session. Embarrassed, Gibson would explain his drawing style and encourage them to refrain from losing their clothes.

Having friends sit as models sounded appealing to Gibson, as he did not have to shell out modeling fees. Before fame arrived, he convinced his brother and close friends from school to pose for his pen. As his work became recognized and association with him brought bragging rights, socialites and mere acquaintances clamored to become part of his portfolio. While he never identified the people he drew, his talent faithfully captured the subject's essence such that they could hold up the published drawing and declare their brush with artistic fame. Claims of being a Gibson Girl ran rampant among social and theatrical sets, some true, some not.

Unidentified model.
Widows and Friends, 1901

However, he soon recognized that using friends and family was often counter-productive. A hired model would come in and sit, as requested, with the proper etiquette of not moving or talking. They were in and out of the studio in an economical amount of time. In contrast, his friends did not have the same discipline, and sessions required all day to accomplish what took a couple hours with a professional. Time was of great value and wasting it was not good business.

• • •

When did she appear? There was no single magical day that she materialized like Eve. The most recognizable Gibson Girl followed many sisters that came before her. In addition, like most younger siblings, she struggled, sometimes rebelliously, to establish herself in the world.

AN OPPORTUNITY FOR A RENAISSANCE
Why these boys? Because men who have work to do in the daytime must go to bed before the morning hours.

An original *cougar* reference.
An Opportunity Renaissance
Life, January 23, 1890

The 1890 *An Opportunity Renaissance* sketch is a century-old take on modern *cougars,* mature women stalking young men. The variety of women shows their beauty within the limited print capabilities of the day. Print quality aside, Gibson's quick wit was already well developed.

The woodcut printing plates of the day limited high-volume prints to crude representations. By the end of 1890, a race was on among publishers to incorporate the latest and best means to print high quality images.[5]

Higher quality printing would be crucial to faithfully producing an image that the public would seize upon. The soon-to-be improvements were as impressive on the printed page as high-definition broadcast is to the modern video experience. The 1889 woodcut with 'Penelope Peachblow' and 'Dolly Flicker' showcases Gibson's artistic ability within restrictions of the current printing technology.

Early woodcut image
Life, May 21, 1889

Miss Penelope Peachblow: I AM SORRY YOU WERE QUITE SO JOLLY, AS IT IS CONSIDERED BAD FORM NOW FOR GIRLS TO DRINK MUCH CHAMPAGNE.
Miss Dolly Flicker: IT MAY BE BAD FORM, BUT IT'S GOOD TASTE.

Soon, his focus on familiar women characters and models came to define much of Gibson's artwork. A few of his favorites can be recognized over months or even years of publications, contributing to the iconic look that is most recognized as the Gibson Girl.

• • •

Which came first? The Gibson Girl look or the look that she adopted? The brilliant and lovable, if not controversial, 19th century poet and playwright, Oscar Wilde offered in 1889, that "life imitates art more than art imitates life."[6] This gem is certainly brought to mind when trying to decide the Gibson Girl's affect on society.

Following Wilde's thought just three years later, George Bernard Shaw wrote in his preface to *Three Plays:* "I have noticed that when a certain type of feature appears in painting and is admired as beautiful, it presently becomes common in nature."[7] Imitation seems to be a significant characteristic of humankind.

Young mid-west women who adopted the Gibson Girl look to perfection.
c. 1902, Emporia, Kansas

The fashion and personality Gibson assigned to his character became increasingly popular with each additional magazine appearance. He did not invent her aura, though he certainly promoted it. A contemporary woman walking down Fifth Avenue in New York may not have been influenced by a dress or social stance in the latest Gibson drawing, but a young woman in the country's heartland might have immediately set a new course of personal style and attitude upon viewing the latest images in *Life* or *Collier's*.

Gibson Girl imitation spanned class and economic lines with ease. The office assistant, store clerk, telephone operator, or secretary could incorporate as much of the look as she could afford or that felt comfortable. Not everyone could look and experience the complete life depicted on magazine pages, yet they could grab a piece of it. The phenomena was probably similar to legions of young girls copying Farrah Fawcett's 1978 feathered hairstyle, sporting a bare midriff in 2001 à la Britney Spears, or now choosing a provocative piece from the Kardashian Kollection.

Well-off society women could afford the cost and spend the time to become a Gibson Girl. Elaborate balls and dinners were the perfect occasion for a head-turning entrance, while fundraisers and charity balls across the country incorporated the Gibson Girl as a party theme

There were so many looks and styles to chose from in Gibson sketches, some feature would have appealed to almost any young debutante. Besides influence from Gibson drawings, magazines such as *Ladies' Home Journal* were replete with fashion articles and advertising that provided further guidance and suggestions to becoming a Gibson Girl.

It appeared that Gibson was dictating or predicting the future of American style and thought. However, his prophecies were not magic, clairvoyant, or even genius. He actually did see the future, metaphorically that is. Just as many people in the era spent considerable time traveling or living in Europe, Gibson visited the old countries frequently, with Paris and London being his favorite destinations.

Dress and hairstyles were conceived in Paris then reproduced around the world. He always captured what he saw on a sketch pad and soon these observations decorated his stylish drawings. Many looks in his artwork may have struck the less-traveled person as original, but actually he was previewing that which soon would land on American shores.

• • •

Who is that girl? Once Gibson became universally recognized for his pop culture success, he was burdened with typical questions from the paparazzi of the day. It seemed every reporter, amateur artist, admirer, and tabloid reader wanted the identity of a specific woman that inspired him. He never used the term "Gibson Girl", and was embarrassed that his work was labeled as such. He usually referred to the artistic phenomenon as the "American Girl" or an "American Type."

In 1910, with his work and reputation at near-legendary heights, a long-time acquaintance interviewed him for a second time; the first was twenty years earlier, well before fame and fortune. Still, the interview with Ed-

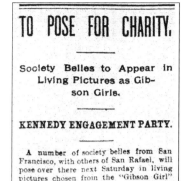

San Francisco Call
July 5, 1895

The *Gibson Girl* popularized the *shirt-waist*, a blouse prototype.

The Education of Mr. Pipp, 1899

ward Marshall of the *New York Times* was uneasy, as Gibson did not like to talk about himself. Marshall pressed him many times trying to uncover some unpublished revelation worthy of a headline.

Possibly because of their old friendship and his respect, Gibson tolerated the line of questioning more than usual as Marshall sat there with only one leg, lost from wounds suffered on San Juan Hill during the Spanish American War. A fearless war correspondent, he was a fellow reporter of Gibson's best friend Richard Harding Davis. With that in mind, Marshall may have received more consideration than many reporters did.

Pressed about the American Type of girl, Gibson finally delved into a philosophical dialogue framed in the artist's world:

> *The idea of the old time European artist, and of many new time artists on the other side, is that women can be just two things - mere toys or mere machines. The Englishman and the American - more notably, of course, the American - see that they are the biggest and best part of life and treat them with regard and wonder. It is this appreciation that has helped our art, more than any other one thing has.*

> *The men who harness women up with dogs will not advance much in their art, the men who place them where they rightfully belong, will really progress. It's all in the conception. Women are the most beautiful of all created things - not women sitting on a cloud, idealized, but honest, living, helping, actual women - women such as we have here in the United States.*[8]

This discussion surely revealed personal values and his respect for women and their deserved rights in the world. Gibson treated women honestly and fairly, though he was brave enough to call out weaknesses or flaws when needed. Thus was the fairness of Gibson satire; it was critically sharp where appropriate, yet kind with praise when deserved.

Warning to Noblemen
Life, May 9, 1903

WARNING TO NOBLEMEN.
TREAT YOUR AMERICAN WIFE WITH KINDNESS.

The philosophical answers were enlightening, but Marshall kept pressing for insight to the Gibson Girl's original identity while his friend and artist persistently dodged the subject. Stunningly, Gibson brought up the subject whilst they were actually engaged in a different topic:

> *I'll tell you how I got what you have called the 'Gibson Girl.' I saw her on the streets, I saw her at the theatres, I saw her in the churches. I saw her everywhere and do everything. I saw her idling on Fifth Avenue and at work behind the counters of the stores. From hundreds, thousands, tens of thousands, I formed my ideal. In starting out in life, each man worth while has his ideal of womanhood. A poet may, perhaps, create his wholly from his fancy. I guess I'm not a poet. I got mine from the crowd.*

Maybe Gibson felt a need to set the record straight, and here was a chance with an old friend he had known since the earliest days at *Life*. Still, even this trusted reporter missed most of the points Gibson was trying to make. The story headline shouted:

THE GIBSON GIRL ANALYZED BY HER ORIGINATOR
Artist Whose Delineation of the Young American Woman Made Him Famous Tells How the Type Came Into Existence and What Her Mission is.

My guess is that Gibson was chagrined upon eyeing the banner. The balance of the story covered Gibson's philosophy on women, men, relationships, respect, and even delved into evolutionary and anthropological analogies to current society. It certainly did not address "What Her Mission" was. Just as today, each individual has a different mission, if any. Gibson's point was the ideal girl attributed to his pen was inspired by thousands of women he had seen, representing millions in the world. So how could there be a singular mission?

Critics are going to criticize. Some historians claim Gibson's drawings and messages were shallow, if not outright sexist. But these experts usually isolate a drawing or two and then define it in a manner that fits their goal. His drawings eventually represented nearly all facets of life, from the simple to the complex. His messages that women could do anything and benefit from their rights were usually subtle and witty. Undeniably, he also liked drawing attractive characters.

• • •

Minnie Clark, a young widow from Washington D.C., was one of Gibson's favorite and most sketched models. She was known for a perfect face structure, not the most beautiful but the most artistic. Today we would call her photogenic. He worked with Minnie as early as 1891, for the *Scribner's* image of her conquering the Sphinx.

William M. Chase, a renowned artist from the era, says of her: "She possesses a beauty which I seldom find."[9] Gibson himself praised her in an 1894 interview as having "blue gray eyes, dark curly hair, a perfect nose and mouth and a faultless figure." The artist in him praised her as the perfect model by adding "she is simply all women in one and can laugh or cry, be awkward or graceful, look stupid, pensive, amused, interested or clever, and all at will."[10]

Untitled Gibson Girl

With those credentials, it is no wonder that Mrs. Clark was in constant demand throughout the art world. She was the model for the Statue of the Republic that stood watch over the entrance to the 1893 Chicago World's Fair. A replica stands in Jackson Park of the same city today. Daniel French reportedly sculpted his well-known figure of *Death and the Sculpture*, also known as the *Angel of Death*, with Mrs. Clark as his model. That relief sculpture graces the Forest Hills Cemetery in Boston.[11]

Minnie Clark sketch by Carrol Beckwith, presented to the Brooklyn Museum in 1917.

Wikimedia Commons

Lessons From The Gibson Girl

DANGER

THE SHORE IS LINED WITH WRECKS.

Danger

Life, June 29, 1893

A confident Minnie Clark walks among the scattered wrecks of love.

Even though Gibson publicly claimed that he worked with a specific model for no more than two consecutive drawings, Minnie Clark's image is recognizable over several years. She started modeling for Gibson during the woodcut era that did not do justice to her and Gibson's drawings. In contrast, as the more elegant photo-mechanical printing process was used, her influence and beauty enhanced his drawings even more.

She possessed the perfect poise for many of Gibson's drawings requiring a strong and confident woman such as in the *Danger* cartoon.

Chapter 4 – The Gibson Girl

Little Susanne is not much of a formal name, unfortunately that is all history provides us. Gibson met this young model and aspiring stage actress while in Paris, and then sponsored her move to New York in 1894. One of her first Gibson appearances was indeed set in France, as a struggling performer, possibly singing for her next meal. Whether the audience felt her performance was worthy of a franc or two, surely the charismatic dog would coax a coin out of a stuffy old woman's purse.

On The Road To Versailles
Life, April 6, 1894

ON THE ROAD TO VERSAILLES.
A PRIMA DONNA'S DEBUT

This slight Parisian, sometimes referred to as *Mademoiselle Susanne*, was a noticeable departure from the domineering presence of Minnie Clark except that her modeling skills were also of the highest caliber.

Lessons From The Gibson Girl

Though exhibiting a young and innocent look, she frequently appeared in serious scenes projecting an emotion integral to the sketch. A reporter in 1894 wrote about her:

> *Studying for the stage helps her to assume the expression and pose necessary for any character. Mr. Gibson tells her the story of the picture he is drawing, and she in her intense sympathy and dramatic imagination, looks the part at once without being conscious of any effort.*[12]

The drawing *No Respecter of a Widow's Grief* reveals the dramatic flair that she could bring to a scene.

No Respecter of a Widow's Grief
Life, October 11, 1894

NO RESPECTER OF A WIDOW'S GRIEF.

Evelyn Nesbit became the quintessential Gibson Girl vision. She has been called America's first super model, appearing on the cover of countless magazines and appearing in advertisements for everything from soap to beer.

She lived a tumultuous life, riddled by tragedies, including a murdered husband, suicide attempts, and a failed stage career. An overly ambitious mother pushed Evelyn into modeling while still a teenager, her true age unknown, but probably in her mid-teens. This success-driven life at any cost left her vulnerable to many unfortunate encounters with people of questionable motives, including a jealous husband and a rich lover.

Evelyn Nesbit
Collier's, April 25, 1905 (l)
Library of Congress (r)

Evelyn Nesbit
Life, September 3, 1903

She came to Gibson's attention before troubles overtook her life. Like many of his best models, she worked on stage as well, a beneficial background. Her images reveal an expert ability to play inspired or requested roles. Even though she was still a teenager, her classic features and acting capabilities enabled Gibson to draw her in many settings, portraying a wide range of maturity and sophistication.

The Gibson Girl personification became crystal clear in his Nesbit drawings. With beauty so evident, her face is attributed to the most reproduced Gibson Girl images, including a U.S. postage stamp appearance eighty year later.

Evelyn Nesbit
Social Ladder, 1902

Famous and near-famous women of the era clamored for a chance to become bona-fide Gibson Girls. Society belles from the arts to politics to simply the wealthy sat for immortalization. Gibson was popular on the society circuit and participated in many charity balls; he was probably cornered at every turn. While he preferred using professional models, his obliging personality may have prevented him from refusing pleading requests from those he knew.

Friends and notables who enjoyed Gibson status included stage stars Ethel Barrymore, the grand-aunt of actress Drew Barrymore, and Maude Adams, the highly successful actress who first portrayed Peter Pan on stage. Taking a little more social risk, Gibson is reported to have drawn Theodore Roosevelt's rebellious daughter, Alice Roosevelt who did resemble many of Gibson's drawings.

Ethel Barrymore (l)
Alice Roosevelt (r)

Library of Congress

A contingent of Philadelphia society women were said to have sat for their fifteen minutes of fame, along with New York celebrities. While the Nesbit-type images are most associated with the Gibson Girl, our popular artist drew endless varieties from the many models, friends, and acquaintances that passed through his studio.

A variety of unidentified models from several table books:

Social Ladder, 1902
The Weaker Sex, 1903
Everyday People, 1904

Chapter 4 – The Gibson Girl

Charles Dana Gibson's portfolio star was a transitional woman in the sense that the world around her was evolving, and she with it. An affluent lifestyle was enriching the lives of workers and shopkeepers. Secondly, women's freedoms and rights were encouraged. And thirdly, the flourishing publishing industry filled magazines with entertaining drawings, stimulating editorials, and adventurous stories.

The era created a perfect storm of change, whereas the Gibson Girl may not have occurred without the confluence of these evolutionary events. "All Broken Up" embodied examples of all three circumstances: the wealth of auto ownership, the woman's expectation to drive it, and the humor magazine to print an exceptionally drawn image.

All Broken Up
Collier's, January 17, 1903

ALL BROKEN UP.
Another collision with serious results.

– 83 –

Unconventional suffragist might be a fitting description of the Gibson Girl. Arguably, she was an important transitional figure in the United States suffrage movement, even though she was a fictional character.

She was emblematic of real suffragists – young educated, independent, and confident women who broke free from the shackles their mothers suffered. The new generation took up the battle flag from the aging and dying stalwarts, bringing more political action to the national suffrage movement.

These new leaders grew up reading the surging media coverage of contemporary issues, including Gibson's social satire. They even embraced and adopted the media to help recast their mission in a character that was less fearful to many.

In Emily Scarborough's exceptional master's thesis, "Fine Dignity, Picturesque Beauty, and Serious Purpose: The Reorientation of Suffrage Media," she observed:

> *Twentieth century suffragists sought to review their image in the public's mind. To do so, they created an identity that played into existing, popular opinions on class, race, and beauty to become mainstream rather than marginal.* [13]

From the pages of popular magazines, the media-savvy Gibson Girl went to war for suffrage in her own subtle way.

Gibson is credited with great influence over society, especially young college students. Possibly one such collegian was Alice Paul who became one of the most important suffrage leaders of the 20th century. Before her thirtieth birthday, she had confronted President Wilson and anti-suffrage politicians with a large Woman Suffrage Procession in Washington – the day before his inauguration. She kept up the fight for suffrage, even enduring arrest and prosecution several years later for picketing the White House.

At the age of sixteen, Alice entered Swarthmore College in Pennsylvania, as a biology major at the height of the Gibson Girl's popularity. She lived and experience a normal and "giddy"[14] life at Swarthmore which is suggestive of a Gibson Girl's imaginary life.

> *She delighted in the athletics so new to women's lives. She overslept some classes. She went to football games when Swathmore played Haverford and to dances with boys.*[15]

Alice enjoyed the freedoms of a Gibson Girl. Perhaps she was encouraged by fictional role models found in popular magazines before becoming one of the most influential suffrage figures of the 20th century.

Alice Paul portrait in a classic Gibson Girl look.
Library of Congress, c. 1915

A prototype of the modern American suffragist, Alice Paul brought an organized, intellectual, and politically aggressive approach to the battle for women's rights. After receiving her degree in biology, Alice earned a Ph.D. in economics, and two law degrees.

A tireless worker, after the 19th Amendment success she worked on several precursors of the Equal Rights Amendment (ERA), which eventually passed congress in 1972. However, only 35 states chose to ratify, leaving the Constitutional change three shy of the required number. Therefore, the ERA is NOT the law of the land.

States that never ratified are: Florida, Illinois, Louisiana, Missouri, North Carolina, Oklahoma, South Carolina, and Virginia.

In a symbolic gesture, Nevada ratified the ERA on March 22, 2017. This was well past the procedural cutoff date of 1982, but the measure is meaningful and is possibly a sense of hope that will spread.

If lessons from the fictional Gibson Girl resonate with people today, the lessons from Alice Paul should be studied as well.

Gibson did not draw suffragists marching down the street, banners stretched between the lead duo and others thrusting 'Women Votes' signs upward to an unsynchronized cadence. That would have been too easy. Besides, there were plenty of cartoonists and critics creating these images – many with not-so-kind depictions. Gibson looked beyond the battle at hand, and saw what could be.

A CABINET MEETING.
WHEN OUR BETTERS RULE.

A Cabinet Meeting
Pictures of People, 1902

His "Cabinet Meeting" illustration probably was not drawn with literal expectations of the future. Maybe it was simply intended to instill in young women who followed the Gibson Girl that anything was possible.

• • •

Chapter 5

The Gibson Man

You could not have a Gibson Girl without a love interest to provide endless story lines and banter. The Gibson Man would join her in sports, dinners, travel, courtship, and of course love.

The handsome partner was her equal in all manners of life including obvious good looks, class, and stature. Yet, beyond the appeal as her admirer and suitor, he too would exhibit weakness, confusion, wants, and needs scattered amongst strengths and dedication.

Frequently her sidekick, focus, or date; he was never the lead actor. The Gibson Girl played the lead in most episodes, he was cast in the supporting role.

Many young women admired this strength and longed to be a Gibson Girl, not just to enjoy the glamorous life, alluring look, and handsome escort, but also to speak their mind and control their destiny.

Their relationship was not written as a serialized story, each cartoon stood on its own merit. A story started and ended in one panel, usually encompassing courtship, a clash or argument, or a love connection. Gibson chose not to dominate one with the other by allowing equally witty teases back and forth, providing entertainment for all readers whether they identified with him or her. It was a continual romance, worthy of interest for two decades.

Gibson Man
Life, May 10, 1900

Lessons From The Gibson Girl

THEIR FIRST QUARREL.
AND THEY HAVE BEEN ENGAGED ABOUT TWENTY MINUTES.

Their First Quarrel
Life, November 2, 1899

Their relationship with its frequent ups and downs was followed and admired by legions of readers. It was not unlike familiar encounters portrayed in the television program *Friends* that entertained millions of viewers for ten years with a continual barrage of emotional and sexual banter.

Who was the Gibson Man? Did this gentrified character actually exist? The answer is similar to the Gibson Girl origins, he existed in many men.

• • •

Chapter 5 – The Gibson Man

Langdon Gibson, Dana's older brother, made occasional appearances as the leading man. He was handsome and could look the part as well as any of the Gibson Men. His mother once commented to her husband, who evidently was a handsome prize also: "Langdon is like you, dear. He'll have a hard time fighting off the girls."[1]

Langdon Gibson
Northward Over The Great Ice,
1898

Langdon in early sketch.
Life, May 13, 1890

His brother may have been an economical convenience for Dana, since Langdon only sat for sketches early in the artist's career. Also, modeling appearances were erratic as he was frequently away exploring exotic locations such as the Grand Canyon or the Arctic regions of Greenland.

In 1894, he married, started a family, and began work at the General Electric Company where he rose to an executive position. The modeling career for the younger brother was short lived, yet he set a high standard for Gibson Men with his admirable character and adventurous spirit.

• • •

James Dekay, a Gibson friend who hailed from his ancestral home in Marion, Massachusetts was an anomaly to most Gibson Man stereotypes. The uniqueness of DeKay was that he was blond and sported a mustache, and was actually more of a society character than Dana or Langdon.

Even though his brother Langdon sported a mustache, Gibson was said to have single-handedly made the mustache disappear from popularity. Gibson typically drew no dashing young men with facial hair – except for his friend DeKay.

James DeKay
Everyday People 1904

Gibson's penchant for a clean-shaven face may have been passed down from his father. His father Charley was without facial hair and claimed that no man with it should be allowed to kiss a child. This little quirk of the elder Gibson seemed to influence Dana's preference for himself and his characters, though the father's edict did not take with Langdon.

Yet James DeKay kept his mustache through years of starring in sketches fitting his social standing. In contrast, other moustached men were usually scoundrels or otherwise unattractive men, sort of the archetypical villain Simon Lagree.

• • •

Chapter 5 – The Gibson Man

Richard Harding Davis is undeniably the most recognized Gibson Man. He was every bit as handsome and desirable as his opposite-sex partner was beautiful. In real life he was even more dashing, heroic, and adventurous than anything Gibson depicted.

Davis was three years older than Gibson and grew up in a home strong in character like his soon to be best friend. His father, Lemuel Clarke Davis, was a Philadelphia newspaper editor and strong abolitionist, his mother was noted author and feminist Rebecca Harding Davis who wrote over 400 novels and countless magazine pieces. Richard inherited their work ethic, strong sense of character, and willingness to fight for what was right.

A young Richard Harding Davis
Richard Harding Davis - His Way

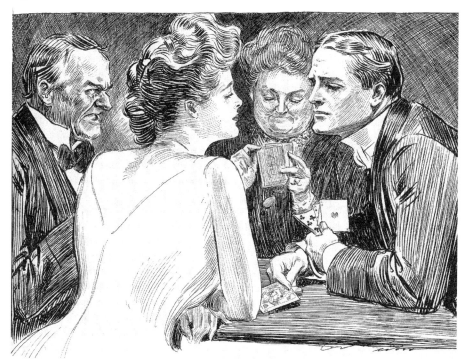

Distracted at Hearts
Collier's, 1903

Though he was a less-than-stellar student at Lehigh University and John Hopkins University, writing was the one area of study he excelled. Continuing his role as a contributor to the school newspapers, he became a reporter for several newspapers in the Philadelphia area. This was a natural career path. His biographer Fairfax Downey noted that Davis was born "with a silver pen in his mouth."[2]

This real life Gibson Man became a celebrated author, reporter, and self-styled man of the world. He could be described as a blend of Sean Connery, Harrison Ford, and Ernest Hemingway with a little Hunter S. Thompson sprinkled on top. Conversely, Davis would have been an influence on all of them as he pre-dated each.

Indeed, a young Hemingway studied Davis' advice in his 1891 story *The Reporter Who Made Himself King*, a primer for young boys on how to become a reporter.[3] Much of Hemingway's war reporting is evocative of Davis' style.

Davis and Gibson both enjoyed strapping good looks and athletic skills that most boys and young men anguish over. Except for over-the-top deeds and a larger-than-life persona that Davis brought to the character, Gibson could have modeled the Gibson Man after himself.

In *Adventures and Letters of Richard Harding Davis*, edited by his brother Charles Belmont Davis after Richard's death, the younger sibling proudly wrote:

> *He was brimming over with physical health and animal spirits and took the keenest interest in every one he met and in everything that was going on about him.*[4]

Known as an aggressive reporter willing to take chances, Davis infiltrated a burglary gang to break a great story and end their criminal activity. After his notes and first-hand experience were shared with local constables, the illegal enterprise was broke apart and the thieves were sentenced to appropriate prison terms.

Richard Harding Davis
From *A Tender Heart*
Life, May 22, 1890

Between his derring-do and everyday reporting, Davis wrote fictional short stories for popular magazines such as *Collier's*, *Life*, and *Harper's*. Nearly every magazine publisher included a book publishing division as part of their business, providing exceptional writers with a path to further exposure and rewards. Best-selling books soon flowed from Harding's pen, usually adventures in exotic locales with himself thinly disguised as the action hero.

Davis recognized that if his career was to grow a move to New York was necessary. In 1889, he took a position in New York with *The Evening Sun* newspaper where his writing improved and his reputation grew. Continuing a rise in literary stature, by the end of 1890 Davis was appointed managing editor of *Harper's Weekly*. *Harper's* was a literary hot spot as Richard's brother wrote "at this time no periodical had a broader or greater influence for the welfare of the country."[5] This was a meteoric rise in Davis' career as he was still a youthful twenty-six years old. Yet sitting behind an editor's desk did not fit Davis' personality, he was a man of action.

A few years later, he represented *Scribner's* magazine in the reporter's pool assigned to cover the conflict with Spain – the matter soon to be called the Spanish-American War. He was on board the battleship U.S.S. New York as it fired the first shots at Cuba on April 15, 1898. Davis recounted the bedlam as:

> *Everybody was sunning, officers, middies, and crew, everyone seemed to have been caught just at the wrong end of the ship on the wrong deck at the exact point farthest from his division.*[6]

His stirring account, published as the lead story in the October 1898 *Scribner's*, aroused his readership's adrenalin and bolstered his reputation. Soon however, the stakes and his reporting became more dangerous as the war moved from the sea to land.

Davis was on San Juan Hill when volunteer forces led by the 9th Colored Unit of the 10th Infantry took the hill, while the Rough Riders led by Teddy Roosevelt supported the charge. It was a withering battle, void of anything romantic. The clarity and bluntness of his words revealed a writing style that gripped a wide audience:

> *They walked to greet death at every step, many of them, as they advanced, sinking suddenly, or pitching forward and disappearing in the high grass, but others waded on, stubbornly, forming a thin blue line that kept creeping higher and higher up the hill.*[7]

Davis' reporting catapulted him into the public's eye as a fearless writer, a fame he capitalized on many times with magazine articles and books.

R. H. Davis spent much of his time chasing battles big and small in far-away lands. The Greco-Turkish War of 1896–97, the South African Boer War in 1900, the Russo-Japanese War in 1904-05, and the Great War, were some of his assignments.

When guns were not pointed at him, he conjured up his own adventures. He and two fellow explorers decided to flee the snow-bound streets of New York of 1895 in *search of warm weather and other unusual things.*[8] They traveled to New Orleans, caught a steamer ship to British Honduras, traveled across Central America to the Pacific Ocean, sailed down the coast to Panama, trekked back across the isthmus to the Atlantic, then boarded another steamer to Caracas. All for the search of unusual things.

This adventure was chronicled in his book *Three Gringos in Venezuela and Central America;* a journey not unlike Hunter Thompson's *Fear and Loathing in Las Vegas* trip, but without hallucinogenic fortification.

Lt. Col. Theodore Roosevelt and Richard Harding Davis at encampment near San Juan Hill.

Library of Congress

Davis relished the limelight of a dashing adventurer and war reporter. The fact that his friend C. D. Gibson made him the heartthrob of women around the world enhanced his allure even further. During this time, R. H. Davis was the *world's most interesting man*.

• • •

During Gibson's 1888 trip to England, he first met Davis in London's Victoria Hotel smoking room. It was a chance encounter, though considering their related professions and intersecting circle of friends, a crossing of paths was inevitable. The happenstance must have been interesting, they had much in common and both were on the ascending slope of their careers. Upon returning to the United States, they reconnected, and the rest as they say is history.

C. D. Gibson and R. H. Davis were predictable pals, their friendship looked like any number of buddy movies portraying two inseparable heroes. Thrown into close proximity in New York by their careers, they were part of the generation that experienced tremendous changes of lifestyles and values. Their friendship went deep; Davis was an usher in Gibson's wedding alongside James DeKay, with Langdon as the best man.

• • •

When not modeling as the Gibson Man, Davis explored the world.
Three Gringos in Venezuela and Central America, 1895.

Gibson Men were not always suave and confident. Like many of us when young, they could be quite awkward, as this dog observes.

Hanging Around Us...
Life, August 15, 1901

The Dog: HERE HE HAS BEEN HANGING AROUND US FOR A MONTH AND WE LEAVE TO-NIGHT

When the Gibson Man did appear to be the successful seducer, upon further inspection, you can usually see a wry smile on the Gibson Girl's face revealing that she actually orchestrated the scenario.

Gibson's leading men portrayed *everyman*, and were more than simply characters on paper – they represented Gibson's observations of them, and quite possibly his own traits as well.

• • •

Chapter 6

Rise To Fame

C. D. Gibson's rise to fame, arm-in-arm with the Gibson Girl, was remarkable in many aspects. His prominence encompassed far more than simply being a stellar artist and successful business man, he was a steadfast friend of many and a respected leader of his peers.

Gibson rose quickly in the illustrator ranks, eventually becoming *Life* magazine's most prolific contributor. Drawing full and double-page cartoons, and prestigious covers gave him unprecedented exposure to a national audience. His humor was sharp and sophisticated especially for an artist of his young age.

He compelled the reader to contemplate a cartoon, and understand his intended lesson or inject their own interpretation. Conversely, the cartoon was sometimes right to the point and solicited an immediate smile.

• • •

Competition among magazine publishers for Gibson's talents eventually reached frenzied levels. Driven by new printing methods that economically produced attractive images, demand swelled for illustrated magazines and newspapers. Top-notch artists such as Gibson were pursued by the leading magazines to satisfy this need.

His stable of clients included *Scribner's*, *Harper's*, *Ladies' Home Journal*, *Collier's*, *Cosmopolitan*, and lesser appearances in nearly every popular journal. Primary allegiance however was with *Life* magazine, the very publication that purchased his first drawing. By the year 1903, over 800 Gibson drawings had appeared in *Life*, from small early cartoons to double-page spreads and countless covers. However, with demand heating up for the best of the best, the rules soon changed in the illustration business.

Charles Dana Gibson Draws Exclusively for Life

Life, January 12, 1899

An 1899 full-page advertisement for Gibson prints and books led with a notice that he drew exclusively for *Life*. This was short lived and may not have been exactly true, as his work is found elsewhere at the time. However, this signaled a bragging and bidding war for his services.

Collier's Weekly was a struggling magazine in the early 1900s, though its fortunes soon changed mostly due to the efforts of one man. Condé Montrose Nast, armed with a prophetic business philosophy, transformed the magazine business and its relationships with artists and writers well before he founded his namesake magazine *Conde Nast*.

In the early 1890s, Nast was a Georgetown University classmate of Robert Collier, son of the magazine founder Peter Collier. After pursing a law degree and then abandoning that effort, Nast fell back to his natural inclination and joined his own family's printing business. Shortly thereafter though, Robert Collier hired his college chum Nast away from his family's business to work for the Collier magazine, where he soon became the advertising manager and then advanced to business manager. Nast brought a commitment to offering nothing but the best to his readers, believing that:

> . . .that top writers and artists attracted readers, so the work of figures such as Upton Sinclair and Frederic Remington appeared on a regular basis.[1]

Not only did these artists and others appear in *Collier's*, Nast attempted to lock them in with exclusive contracts. He was successful with many leading artists, including Remington who produced some of his finest western-themed paintings for double-page spreads. Nast wanted Gibson also.

Collier's enticed Gibson to join them for $1,000 a drawing for ten drawings on an exclusive basis. Already understanding his popularity and having the leverage and negotiating skills, Gibson countered with a larger number of drawings and a non-exclusive deal, leading to even more bargaining.

After negotiations fell through for exclusive rights to Gibson, *Collier's* agreed to share him with *Life*. In a handwritten note, Gibson accepted the world's most expensive artist contract at the time. Three months later, *Collier's* proudly published the contract in their weekly magazine.[2] The note simply read:

> P. F. Collier and Son
>   Dear Sir
>   I hereby accept your offer of $100,000 for 100 double page cartoons to be delivered to you during the next four years. And I agree to draw only for "Colliers Weekly" and "Life"
>   Sincerely yours
>   C. D. Gibson

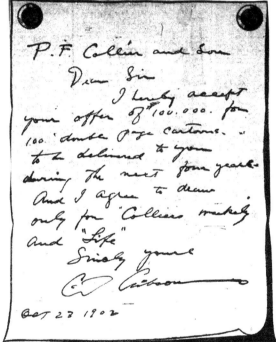

Handwritten note from Gibson to P.F. Collier accepting world's highest drawing offer.
Collier's Weekly, February 7, 1903

Christmas Time
Collier's, December 24, 1904

The magnitude of this agreement is revealed when viewed in today's dollar-value. A calculation using the Consumer Price Index reveals the contract was equal to nearly three million dollars in current value (2016)[3]. The terms worked out to $28,000 each if drawn today. Since this was not an exclusive contract, Gibson was free to not only produce cartoons for *Life*, and continue developing his own art books and other products.

Gibson drew some his finest work for *Collier's*, including these heart-touching scenes of a compassionate Gibson Girl in December of 1904.

CHRISTMAS TIME

Chapter 6 – Rise to Fame

The December 24, 1904 *Collier's* issue portrayed the care a well-to-do woman brought to a family of obvious sad means. Her driver proudly brings in food and needed items, maybe a toy for the child. Perhaps, this sketch would encourage readers to extend some charity of their own.

In the very next issue for New Year's Eve, he combines the metaphor of a *new year* with the inevitable fate of death attempting to claim one of the couple as its own – futilely held back by a protective cupid.

AN INTERRUPTED STORY

The combination of compelling sketches and patented micro-stories of love and life, kept his popularity ever growing towards greater fame.

• • •

An Interrupted Story
Collier's, December 31, 1904

Erotica and action stories provided Charles Dana Gibson with opportunities to venture away from the stereotype antics of the Gibson Girl and become a sought-after illustrator of a hot genre. The Gibson Girl now became a more complex character in his portfolio.

Illustrating novels and short stories gave Gibson new creative challenges, and introduced his fans to different facets of his talent.

Early in his career, *Scribner's* offered Gibson the chance to illustrate a short story by Sarah Orne Jewett, a respected author with numerous published books and stories in her portfolio. *The Luck of the Bogans,* a twelve-page short story with three Gibson illustrations, was published in the January 1889 edition of *Scribner's Magazine.* Given an illustration assignment for such an established author was endorsement of Gibson's skill. Though he was still a struggling artist with limited exposure, this project would portend his rise to prominence.

"Illustrated by . . ." could also help boost sales if the illustrator was well-known and respected, as some readers sought books that included artwork by their favorite artist. Valuable promotions included listing the illustrator on the book cover or jacket, and mentions in related advertising. The quality of accompanying drawings was always important, but an author also wanted an artist that could accurately portray a scene or character of the book. Charles Dana Gibson was a master at visually representing the character.

A successful story illustrator, whether drawing for a short story or a lengthy novel, needed several talents beyond the ability to draw pretty pictures. The artist needed to understand the story as the author meant and translate it into visual images. He also needed to be a costume designer. The writer's description may have been ". . . obviously a beggar wearing tattered rags that, hung off his boney frame." The artist would need to create a vision of those clothes and the emaciated man. The illustrator was also a director and make-up artist, giving the subject a personal look and pose fitting of the scene. Finally, the outcome of these talents needed to flow through his hand to paper. Gibson excelled at these demanding requisites as well as any illustrator.

Soon, novelists and book publishers chased him with offers to illustrate their latest works. Novels of the time frequently included six to ten drawings, helping the reader visualize a story line. Just as important, these pictures helped increase a book's sales. Richard Harding Davis asserted that:

> *. . . if one my books sold ten copies without illustrations, it would sell twenty when illustrated by Gibson.*[4]

Adventure novels and stories were the most popular genre around the turn of the century. Wars, exotic or untamed lands always provided exciting backdrops for ever-present human conflict of greed, family battles, love, or adventure. These of course are timeless story lines, as George Lucas of *Star Wars* fame recently discussed his films and explained their success,

> *People don't realize it's actually a soap opera and it's all about family problems – it's not about spaceships.*[5]

Many of the best selling stories one hundred years ago embodied the same concept Lucas referenced – that is, people were more important than places and events. This opened opportunities for good illustrators that could add depth to a story with expressive character images.

No contemporary author captured the spirit of adventure-seeking readers better than Gibson's best friend, Richard Harding Davis. Indeed, Davis entwined love stories and human conflict with diverse settings such as the crime-ridden back streets of Philadelphia in *Gallegher* and the jungles of South America in *Soldiers of Fortune*. *Gallegher,* Davis' first acclaimed publication, earning him a whopping $175 from *Scribner's* in 1890 for a serialized version of the story. Not

Drawings, 1894

only was that a seminal work by Davis, his author-mother wrote "I am so glad I could cry." It was the first of many collaborative projects with Gibson, both of their stars began to shine brighter about the same time.[7]

Gibson illustration for Richard Harding Davis novel.

Gallegher, 1890

Close behind adventure stories in popularity, *erotica* came from behind the book counter and was prominently displayed to catch a shopper's attention. Mainstream publishers did not hesitate to issue quality erotic work by respected authors, especially if the story was illustrated by a highly regarded artist.

Three years after illustrating *Gallegher* and a couple more Davis books, Gibson drew touching scenes for Julia Magruder's suggestive book of mystery, love, and desire set in a Paris art community.

Magruder was a late 19th century writer who questioned traditional roles of women, and championed their ability to join with other women, in various manners, to achieve heights that had been the near-exclusive realm of men.

Gibson needed to dig beyond his customary characterizations of flirtatious love to interpret the sensual atmosphere delivered in *Princess Sonia*. The story of a plain American girl seduced by an alluring Russian princess was set in a respected Paris art school that was known for strict separation of budding artists regardless of their social position.

"OH, I AM SO, SO SORRY."

Oh, I Am So, So Sorry
Princess Sonia, 1895

Gibson perhaps was attracted to Magruder's book as the setting in a Paris *atelier*, or workshop, was reminiscent of his experience nine years prior. These small workshops were popular destinations of American art students attracted to the history, character, and hopefully expert tutelage of French masters. Most ateliers were located in the Left Bank area of Paris, which also encompassed the Latin Quarter. This popular haunt of artists, musicians, philosophers, and other intelligentsia was the center of free-flowing life and eclectic philosophies. What better scene was there for Gibson to study humankind for inclusion in future sketches?

Magruder's words were suggestive, yet clear as to the characters' thoughts and intentions. Her writing skills did not require deliberate or crass narratives to arouse the anxious lovers and indeed the reader. Taking a cue from

"IT WILL BE QUITE SAFE, I SEE"

Book Illustration,
Princess Sonia, 1895

the author's style, Gibson employed this restrained approach in his drawings. Just as arousal is increased by what you do not see, Gibson's artwork in *Princess Sonia* was perfectly matched to the words, leaving the reader to fill in imaginative detail as they wished.

The Gibson and Magruder collaboration delivered not only a vehicle for *new-woman* messages of the time, but the books were also commercial successes. What's more, they are the subject of historical and social research even in the 21st century.

In Melissa R. Pompili's 2013 English Literature master's thesis titled *Transatlantic Intimacies: The Homoerotic Affect Worlds of Nineteenth-Century Print Culture*, Ms. Pompili delved into changing thoughts and motives of many women as reflected in then-current female author writings. Pompili offered:

> *Julia Magruder was without a doubt aiming to be included as one of these new women writers as evidenced by the themes present in her work and her affiliation with Gibson's illustrations, which were culturally aligned with the changing cultural expression of femininity.*

A year after *Princess Sonia* was published, Gibson teamed with Magruder on a follow-up novel, *The Violet*. Pompili reinforces the idea that Gibson brought intelligence and sensitivity to the subject by suggesting his:

> *. . . illustrations work in tandem with Magruder's fiction to draw predominantly female readers from the United States and England into an intimate public in order to build an affective community with one another.[7]*

Illustrating these and other stories during Gibson's early years helped drive recognition of his talents, though these assignments probably did not generate great financial rewards. Ironically, twenty years later he would become a highly paid, respected and in-demand artist by a new generation of best-selling novelists.

His ability to convey emotion in accompanying drawings was a tremendous asset to a book – and its sales.

I Heard Her Sobs
Rupert of Hentzau
by Anthony Hope,
McClure's, April, 1898

• • •

Brand marketing is something everyone in the 21st century can relate to, especially parents of fad-aware children. However, the phenomena did not start with *Star Wars* light sabres and action figures, Minion toys, or even Roy Rogers lunch boxes sixty years ago. These were all late comers to the art of separating you from your money by brand association.

The Gibson Girl brand was a business and commercial juggernaut. Products included calendars, collector prints, wallpaper, chinaware, fans, pillows, carvings, and postcards, anything that could hold an image.

Much to Gibson's frustration, these very products became a double-edge sword. They helped make him very wealthy, yet conspired to put him in

Calendar Ad
Life, November 8, 1900

China Plaques Ad
Life, February 4, 1904

a box he did not relish. He was typecast in a similar manner that certain actors are only offered roles they have played successfully before. Most people associate Gibson almost exclusively with the Gibson Girl.

Table books, with their large format, were as important in creating the Gibson image, as his weekly cartoons. Once a magazine was read, it was most likely discarded, though a Gibson double-page drawing was frequently removed and proudly pinned to a dormitory or apartment wall.

However, for those who wished to collect the artwork, they could anxiously await next year's table book that included high quality, large format prints of the year's best cartoons. Printed on heavy paper these were proudly displayed in sitting rooms and libraries across the country. During the height of his popularity, Gibson and his publishers produced eleven yearly books that became a must-have item in the home of anyone that was aware of the latest trends or wanted to impress visitors.

Seventeen inch-wide bound *table books* with approximately eighty drawings each were issued yearly from 1894 to 1905.

For true collectors, the publisher also produced a two-volume set of all the individual table books. Just as movie aficionados collect the complete set of Star Wars movies and many readers take pride in their Danielle Steel book collection, Gibson's fans could enjoy his complete works in their own home.

The World was hers. It is said that every college dormitory, men's and women's, were festooned with the occupants' favorite Gibson drawing. Men admired the beautiful Gibson Girl images while women enjoyed the style and strength of the Gibson Girl in addition to her handsome men.

Gibson enjoyed audiences with Kings and Queens, Presidents, and various rulers-for-life around the world. He traveled in style on chartered yachts, yet journeyed by donkey and camel to visit Egyptian temples at Karnak and other remote treasures. He dined and bedded in the finest accommodations, yet preferred the solace of his 700-acre Maine island where he labored on most of the structures himself.

Irene Gibson visiting Karnak Temples in Egypt.
Sketches in Egypt, 1899

Richard Harding Davis, a world traveler himself, recounted in a 1905 article:

> *Editors send me all over the world. I find where I go Dana's pictures. In Yokohoma [Japan] I found his books used to fill double window displays. The King and Queen of England when they were the Prince and Princess of Wales, purchased his pictures in the Strand. I have seen them decorating the palm leaf shacks in Central America. In Durban South Africa, I have seen them stuck on the walls of houses.*[8]

Gibson understood the varieties of human nature, and then faithfully described them to millions of readers worldwide. His fame is timeless, as is the Gibson Girl who still garners attention and acclaim today.

● ● ●

Chapter 7

A Lesson Gallery

This gallery showcases Gibson's satirical interpretation of a variety of subjects, nearly all starring a Gibson Girl, or even a group of them. She was not confined to one particular personality or even age. However her frequent appearances during three decades enables grouping of similar subjects for interesting viewing.

The fascinating nature of his drawings is that their humor and relevance is timeless. What was funny, sad, or ironic then – still offers a lesson now.

- ◊ Cupid at Work
- ◊ Snarky Repartee
- ◊ Flirting & Courtship
- ◊ Death Do Us Part
- ◊ Marriage of Contrivance
- ◊ Girls Just Gotta Have Fun
- ◊ Proposals of Sorts
- ◊ Daughters and Sons
- ◊ Kids Say the Darndest
- ◊ True Love
- ◊ Politics
- ◊ Society at Large
- ◊ Marital Bliss
- ◊ For Love of Mutt
- ◊ Second Thoughts
- ◊ Careers Moves
- ◊ On the Edge
- ◊ Domestics

Charles Dana Gibson
Ladies' Home Journal,
October 1902

(The illustrations are reproduced with original words, spelling, and punctuation.)

Lessons From The Gibson Girl
Cupid at Work

Cupid at Work

A significant number of Gibson drawings used Cupid as a protagonist in love scenarios. Cupid was an asexual cherub with bow and arrows close at hand, usually flashing a mischievous grin. *He* or *she*, could be tender, helpful, antagonistic, or even cruel sometimes.

The Story of His Life
Life, December 26, 1901

THE STORY OF HIS LIFE

Chapter 7 – A Lesson Gallery
Cupid at Work

THE INVINCIBLE ARMY

The Invincible Army
Americans, 1900

Lessons From The Gibson Girl
Cupid at Work

Cupid plainly becoming tired while waiting for her answer – to a proposal?

Collier's, August 21, 1909

WAITING HER ANSWER

Chapter 7 – A Lesson Gallery
Cupid at Work

HIS EVERLASTING EXPERIMENTS WITH ILL-MATED PAIRS.

Cupid was not always successful with *his* efforts at fostering love. Yes, Gibson did refer to a masculine cupid in this cartoon, perhaps a habit from his era. While many cupids, particularly in singular appearances, appeared as male, when more than one was in the scene there were clearly girl cupids also.

His Everlasting Experiments With Ill-Mated Pairs.
Drawings, 1904

Lessons From The Gibson Girl
Cupid at Work

Thanksgiving issue cover
Life, November 5, 1903

Chapter 7 – A Lesson Gallery

Cupid at Work

The Expert: WHAT MAKES YOU THINK SHE HAS ONE? I CAN HEAR NOTHING.

What Makes You Think She Has One?
Life, August 29, 1901

Lessons From The Gibson Girl
Snarky Repartee

Snarky Repartee – Gibson armed his leading lady with a quick wit and a sharp tongue – used when required. He empowered her with eloquence that most readers wished they had the nerve or wit to pull off such retorts.

Why Did You Let Me Make Love To You...

Life, April 18, 1901

He: WHY DID YOU LET ME MAKE LOVE TO YOU IF YOU KNEW IT WAS HOPELESS?
"BUT I DIDN'T KNOW IT WAS HOPELESS UNTIL AFTER YOU HAD MADE LOVE TO ME."

Chapter 7 – A Lesson Gallery
Snarky Repartee

How Is Your Kindergarten . . .
Life, November 23, 1893

Elderly Suitor (sarcastically): HOW DOES YOUR KINDERGARTEN GET ON, MISS BLACK?
Miss Black (sweetly): WELL, IT IS BETTER THAN RUNNING AN OLD MAN'S HOME.

Taking No Chances
Life, March 25, 1897

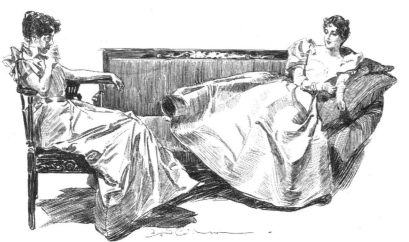

TAKING NO CHANCES
"IT'S VERY STRANGE HE COMMITTED SUICIDE BECAUSE I REFUSED HIM."
"PERHAPS HE WAS AFRAID YOU MIGHT CHANGE YOUR MIND."

Lessons From The Gibson Girl

Snarky Repartee

He Called Me a Colossal Ass...
Life, February 18, 1897

"HE CALLED ME A COLOSSAL ASS!"
"WELL, YOU **are** LARGE."

Chapter 7 – A Lesson Gallery
Snarky Repartee

LEAP YEAR
He: YOU NEVER COMPLIMENT ME ANY MORE ON MY APPEARNCE.
She: OH, CHARMING! CHARMING! CHARMING

Leap Year

Gibson occasionally drew a cartoon labeled as *Leap Year*, where the situation was reversed from a usual scenario.

Life, September 14, 1916

Lessons From The Gibson Girl
Snarky Repartee

A DISPOSITION

He: YOU'LL HAVE TO GO A LONG WAY BEFORE YOU WILL MEET ANYONE WHO LOVES YOU MORE THAN I.
She: WELL, I'M WILLING TO.

A Disposition
Life, October 10, 1901

Chapter 7 – A Lesson Gallery
Snarky Repartee

"YOUNG MAN, HAVE YOU BEEN TRYING TO KISS MY DAUGHTER?"
"NO SIR! I'VE BEEN TRYING *NOT* TO."

. . . Trying to Kiss My Daughter?
Life, September 7, 1905

Lessons From The Gibson Girl

Snarky Repartee

Dig Up The Past...
Life, May 31, 1900

He: YES DEAREST, I HAVE LOVED BEFORE WE MET; BUT LET US NOT DIG UP THE PAST. OH, ALL RIGHT, THEN; IF YOU DON'T WANT TO DIG UP THE PAST, WHY LET'S NOT DIG UP THE FUTURE EITHER.

Chapter 7 – A Lesson Gallery

Snarky Repartee

I Know That You . . .
Life, May 7, 1903

She: "I KNOW THAT YOU MUST HAVE MADE LOVE BEFORE TO SOME OTHER GIRL."
"BUT I HAD YOU IN MIND ALL THE TIME."

Lessons From The Gibson Girl
Flirting & Courtship

Flirting and Courtship – One of Gibson's favorite subjects was all the preliminaries to love. Courtship could be initiated by either, usually surprising the other.

HE GOES TO THE PLAY, BUT FINDS IT IMPOSSIBLE TO BECOME INTERESTED IN THE PIECE.

He Goes To the Play . . .
Collier's, September 26, 1902

Chapter 7 – A Lesson Gallery
Flirting & Courtship

Asking for Kiss Unnecessary...
Life June 21, 1900

She: IF I LET YOU KISS ME THIS ONCE, WILL YOU PROMISE NEVER TO ASK ME AGAIN?
He: CERTAINLY, DEAR, IF YOU CONSIDER IT UNNECESSARY.

Lessons From The Gibson Girl
Flirting & Courtship

SIGNS OF SPRING

Signs of Spring
Our Neighbors, 1904

A Little Incident
Life, May 3, 1900

A LITTLE INCIDENT

– 128 –

Chapter 7 – A Lesson Gallery
Flirting & Courtship

...Riding the Wheel..
Life, August 19, 1897

"IS IT ANY FUN GETTING A MAN TO TEACH YOU HOW TO RIDE THE WHEEL?"
"FUN! WHY. I'VE BEEN TAUGHT THREE TIMES."

Lessons From The Gibson Girl
Flirting & Courtship

Good For One ....
Life, June 15, 1893

"THERE IS NO HARM IN A SUMMER FLIRTATION," SAYS MANY A YOUNG MAN.
BUT WHAT IS FAIR FOR ONE IS FAIR FOR THE OTHER.

Chapter 7 – A Lesson Gallery
Flirting & Courtship

The Busy Wire

Busy Wire
Life, July 7, 1921

Untitled
Life, April 15, 1897

– 131 –

Lessons From The Gibson Girl
Flirting & Courtship

THE SUPPER

SHALL IT BE WHAT SHE IS ACCUSTOMED TO OR THE BEST HE CAN AFFORD?

The Supper
Life, November 30, 1899

Chapter 7 – A Lesson Gallery
Flirting & Courtship

The Young One: I BEG YOUR PARDON, SIR, BUT I BELIEVE IT IS MY TURN NEXT.

As the young man checks the impending change to 1894, Gibson penned a more salacious version of ushering in the New Year, forgoing the typical New Year's baby and an exiting Father Time.

I Beg Your Pardon Sir . . .
Life, January 4, 1894

Lessons From The Gibson Girl

Death Do Us Part

Death Do Us Part – Not of the gruesome sort, more of a light look at its relationship with marriage.

Bishop Gullem: YOU MUSTN'T GRIEVE TOO MUCH, MY DEAR SISTER. REMEMBER THAT THOUGH YOUR DEAR HUSBAND HAS LEFT HIS MORTAL BODY HE IS STILL WITH YOU.
"THAT ISN'T GOING TO AFFECT THE INSURANCE, IS IT?"

Affect The Insurance?
Life, September 5, 1895

Chapter 7 – A Lesson Gallery

Death Do Us Part

Mrs. J. Brassey Pushe: I CONFESS I'M DYING TO GET MY DAUGHTER MARRIED.
The Brute: ER — WHAT OTHER INDUCEMENTS DO YOU OFFER?

Dying to get my daughter married
Life, January 18, 1900

Lessons From The Gibson Girl
Death Do Us Part

Expect a Happy Marriage...?
Life, February 4, 1892

THE ART OF MATRIMONY
"DO YOU EXPECT YOUR MARRIAGE TO BE A HAPPY ONE DEAR?"
"O YES; I GUESS SO. BUT IF IT ISN'T, JACK HAS PROMISED EITHER A DIVORCE OR SUICIDE, SO YOU SEE I'M REALY NOT RUNNING MUCH RISK."

Chapter 7 – A Lesson Gallery
Death Do Us Part

Skinflint: IF ANYTHING SHOULD HAPPEN TO ME, DEAREST, YOU WILL BE ALL RIGHT. I'VE JUST INSURED MY LIFE.
"BUT SUPPOSE NOTHING DOES HAPPEN TO YOU?"

Just Insured My Life . . .
Life, April 14, 1904

Lessons From The Gibson Girl

Marriage of Contrivance

Marriage of Contrivance – Gibson probably drew more social cartoons about this subject than any other. Whether the marriage was to gain a royal title from European aristocrats, or gain financial standing from a mismatched mate, he tried to draw the follies of such unions.

AMERICA'S TRIBUTE.

America's Tribute
Life, March 6, 1890

The lion has represented England for centuries, and is frequently part of family crests and other artwork. In this early drawing on the subject of foreign marriages Gibson used a Coliseum-like arena for the offering of America's most valuable treasures to the English royalty.

Chapter 7 – A Lesson Gallery

Marriage of Contrivance

Papa's check will pay for our wedding trip.
Life, April 6, 1905

She: LOOK DEAR! PAPA'S CHECK WILL PAY FOR OUR WEDDING TRIP.
The Duke: BUT WHAT ARE WE GOING TO DO AFTERWARDS?

Lessons From The Gibson Girl
Marriage of Contrivance

She: PAPA IS GOING TO SETTLE A MILLION ON US.
The Baron: THAT'S WELL. NOW I CAN GIVE YOU A SUITABLE ALLOWANCE.

... *A Million on Us.*
Life, December 4 1902

HONEYMOON
THE MAN WHO MARRIED FOR A HOME

Honeymoon
Life, September 6, 1901

Chapter 7 – A Lesson Gallery
Marriage of Contrivance

Lessons From The Gibson Girl
Marriage of Contrivance

EVERYTHING IN THE WORLD THAT MONEY CAN BUY.

Everything Money Can Buy...
Life, May 23, 1901

Chapter 7 – A Lesson Gallery
Marriage of Contrivance

If the Duke Proposes…
Life, April 13, 1905

Lessons From The Gibson Girl
Girls Just Gotta Have Fun

Girls Just Gotta Have Fun – With three sisters and four sisters-in-law, along with hanging out with his rat-pack-like women friends, Gibson enjoyed a first-hand education of the opposite sex. With these influences, he empowered female characters in his cartoons with strengths and options that broke many taboos and traditions of the past.

The cartoon is suggestive of singer Cyndi Lauper's 1983 signature hit song *Girls Just Want to Have Fun*.

Girls Will Be Girls
Life, July 1, 1897

GIRLS WILL BE GIRLS

Chapter 7 – A Lesson Gallery
Girls Just Gotta Have Fun

THE NIGHT BEFORE HER WEDDING

In case anyone thought the *bachelorette* party was only a recent affair, it has been a tradition for more than one hundred years.

The Night Before Her Wedding
Life, October 28, 1897

Lessons From The Gibson Girl
Girls Just Gotta Have Fun

THE STORY OF THE HUNT.

The Story of the Hunt
Harper & Sons, 1898

She Goes for a Ride
Widow and Her Friends, 1901

Chapter 7 – A Lesson Gallery
Girls Just Gotta Have Fun

"I OFTEN WONDER WHY YOU DON'T GET MARRIED."
"BECAUSE I'M TOO FOUND OF MEN'S SOCIETY."

... Why You Don't Get Married.
Life, December 28, 1899

Cameo Drawings
Widows and Friends, 1901

Lessons From The Gibson Girl
Proposals of Sorts

Proposal of Sorts - Gibson treated the many successful and bumbled proposals with humor and dignity, usually. The traditional preliminary to marriage certainly gave him plenty of material to work with.

Of Course You Can Tell ...
Life, May 10, 1900

OF COURSE YOU CAN TELL FORTUNES WITH CARDS
For instance, if the Jack of Clubs comes between the four and the ten of Diamonds, and the following card happens to be the deuce of Spades, it means that the next offer of marriage should be accepted.

Chapter 7 – A Lesson Gallery
Proposals of Sorts

LIFE'S VAUDEVILLE
"I'LL BE A SISTER TO YOU"

I'll Be a Sister to You

Not all proposals are successful; the dog appears uncomfortable as well.

Life, December 15, 1904

Lessons From The Gibson Girl
Proposals of Sorts

A Last Rememberance
Life, July 9, 1903

A LAST REMEMBERANCE

Ethel (ecstatically): "OH, CHARLIE, WOULD YOU JUST AS LEAVE PROPOSE ALL OVER AGAIN, AND DO IT INTO THIS PHONOGRAPH?"

Cholly: "WHY?"

Ethel: "WHY, I WANT TO HAVE SOMETHING TO REMEMBER YOU BY AFTER YOU HAVE GONE IN AND SPOKEN TO PAPA ABOUT IT."

Chapter 7 – A Lesson Gallery
Proposals of Sorts

HIS BEGINNING.
"I HAD NO IDEA THAT YOU WERE IN LOVE WITH ME."
"NEITHER HAD I, UNTIL I PROPOSED AND YOU REJECTED ME."

His Beginning
Life, August 23, 1900

"IS YOUR ENGAGEMENT A SECRET?"
" OH, NO. THE GIRL KNOWS IT."

Is Your Engagement a Secret . . .
Life, December 8, 1904

– 151 –

Lessons From The Gibson Girl
Proposals of Sorts

The Man I Marry...

Life, Christmas Issue, 1902

The Rich Widow: THE MAN I MARRY MUST BE ONE I CAN RELY ON, TO TAKE CHARGE OF MY ESTATE, AND PROTECT MY INTERESTS.

He: HOW FORTUNATE WE MET!

Chapter 7 – A Lesson Gallery
Proposals of Sorts

...Last Time...
Life, February 26, 1903

The Persistent Suitor (desparately): THIS IS THE LAST TIME I SHALL ASK YOU TO BE MY WIFE.
"OH, THIS IS SO SUDDEN!"

"BILKINS HAS JUST RETURNED."
"WHERE HAS HE BEEN?"
"TO MONTE CARLO, TO WIN ENOUGH TO PAY HIS WEDDING EXPENSES."
"AND THE WEDDING?"
"HAS BEEN POSTPONED FOR TWO YEARS."

Bilkins has returned...
Life, February 25, 1897

Lessons From The Gibson Girl
Daughters and Sons

Daughters and Sons always presented delicious settings for parents and family. Many wonderful jabs were taken at challenging children.

Did I See You Kissing My Daughter...
Life, October 20, 1904

"DID I SEE YOU KISSING MY DAUGHTER, SIR?"
"I REALLY DON'T KNOW SIR, I WAS TOO MUCH OCCUPIED AT THE TIME TO NOTICE."

Chapter 7 – A Lesson Gallery
Daughters and Sons

A Discreet Approach
Life, November 20, 1902

A DISCREET APPROACH.
"ADVISE ME, UNCLE JACK."
"OF COURSE; WHAT IS IT?"
"SHALL I ASK YOU FOR TWENTY-FIVE DOLLARS, OR FOR FIFTY?"

Lessons From The Gibson Girl
Daughters and Sons

Education Cost Me Ten ...
Life, August 25, 1904

The Father: "YOUNG MAN, DO YOU REALIZE THAT YOUR COLLEGE CAREER HAS COST ME TEN THOUSAND DOLLARS?"
"WELL, GOVERNOR, IT WAS WORTH IT."

Chapter 7 – A Lesson Gallery
Daughters and Sons

HIS ONLY CHILD
MR. DOTY'S LITTLE SCHEME FOR RETAINNG HIS DAUGHTER.

His Only Child
Life, Christmas Issue, 1898

Lessons From The Gibson Girl
Kids Say the Darndest

Kids Say the Darndest – Growing up with younger sisters and eventually having children of his own gave Dana Gibson frequent opportunities to observe the unexpected. Even the youngest characters he drew were blessed with the unmistakable Gibson Girl wit, charm, and honesty.

What's That Place Sister?

Life, October 22, 1914

At the time, the Woolworth building in New York City was the tallest building in the world.

"WHAT'S THAT PLACE, SISTER?"
"THAT'S ST. PATRICK'S CATHEDRAL."
"IS HE A BIGGER MAN THAN WOOLWORTH?"

Chapter 7 – A Lesson Gallery
Kids Say the Darndest

Little Sister: A WIDOW? WHAT'S A WIDOW?
Big Sister: A LADY WHAT'S HAD A HUSBAND AND IS GOIN' TO HAVE ANOTHER.

What's a Widow?
Life, April 11, 1915

Lessons From The Gibson Girl

Kids Say the Darndest

Broken the Eighth Commandment...
Life, December 16, 1915

"BOBBY, DO YOU KNOW YOU'VE DELIBERATELY BROKEN THE EIGHTH COMMANDEMENT BY STEALING JAMES' CANDY?"

"WELL, I THOUGHT I MIGHT AS WELL BREAK THE EIGHTH COMMANDMENT AND HAVE THE CANDY, AS TO BREAK THE TENTH AND ONLY 'COVET' IT."

Chapter 7 – A Lesson Gallery
Kids Say the Darndest

Generous
Life, August 12, 1897

GENEROUS
"GIVE ME A BITE OF YOUR CANDY, PLEASE, FLOOSIE?"
"NO, BUT YOU MAY KISS ME WHILE MY MOUF IS STICKY."

Lessons From The Gibson Girl
True Love

True Love – Love scenes were a Gibson favorite – and he drew them well. Few illustrators expressed such a range of emotions, including romance, as well as Charles Dana Gibson.

Who Cares?
Life, July 18, 1901

Chapter 7 – A Lesson Gallery
True Love

Untitled,
Pictures of People, 1896
Gibson readers were occasionally left to imagine the dialog themselves.

Lessons From The Gibson Girl

True Love

WORSHIPERS

Worshipers
Life, March 27, 1902

This drawing appeared in the Easter issue, with an interesting twist that the reader is left to determine.

Chapter 7 – A Lesson Gallery
True Love

ANOTHER MONOPOLY

Another Monopoly
LIfe, November 23, 1899

Lessons From The Gibson Girl

True Love

A SENSELESS AFTER-DINNER CUSTOM.
SO THINKS THE YOUNG MAN WHO MUST LISTEN TO HER FATHER'S FRIENDS DURING THE NEXT HOUR.

A Senseless After-Dinner Custom
Life, November 15, 1899

Chapter 7 – A Lesson Gallery
True Love

THE TURNING OF THE TIDE.

The Turning of the Tide
Life, August 8, 1901

Lessons From The Gibson Girl
Politics

Politics – The art and arena of politics, including suffrage, has not changed much from the Gibson Girl era. Men dominated politics and women were not held up as the leaders or potential leaders of the country.

THE AGITATOR
"Who is it's brought us here, I ask you? Who's a-grindin us under the iron heel o'despotism?
I say to you the time as come, when —"

The Agitator
Collier's, March 11, 1905

Chapter 7 – A Lesson Gallery
Politics

A SCENE IN THE MORAL FUTURE.
WHEN THE SUGGESTIVE REFORMERS SHALL HAVE 'PURIFIED' AMERICA AND 'LIFE'
ALONE REFUSES TO BE COMSTOCKIANIZED.

This political cartoon is tied to controversies of the late 19th century, in particular to one divisive politician, Anthony Comstock.

Comstock pursued his personal brand of censorship and convinced congress to follow. The 'Comstock Act' of 1873 provided for U. S. Postal System censorship and criminal penalties with its ominous title: *Suppression of Trade in, and Circulation of, Obscene Literature and Articles of Immoral Use*. This included birth control information and 'immoral' books. He went on to become the U. S. Postal Inspector where he reportedly caught the approving eye of J. Edgar Hoover, future Director of the FBI.

The cartoon above shows every animal, even birds and squirrels, in the future wearing pants or dresses as a result of extreme *Comstockian* laws.

Moral Future

One of Gibson's earliest cartoons exhibits his creativity and imagination.

Life, January 12, 1888

Lessons From The Gibson Girl
Politics

When Women Vote
MRS. JONES IS OFFICIALLY NOTIFIED OF HER ELECTION AS SHERIFF.

When Women Vote
Life, October 28 1916

Chapter 7 – A Lesson Gallery
Politics

"Hurrah for Teddy!"

Gibson's sketch accompanied an editorial by William Jennings Bryan on the return of ex-President Theodore Roosevelt from a fifteen-month tour of Africa where he hunted big game, and Europe where he gave big speeches. He was treated like a returning hero as the country had missed his larger than life personality. Tickets to Pier A in New York were required to witness his arrival.

Hurrah for Teddy
Collier's, June 18, 1910

Lessons From The Gibson Girl
Society at Large

Society at Large - Gibson drew many cartoons that were just observations of life. They bring value to historians by showng the variety of people that surrounded the Gibson Girl.

Brothers
Our Neighbors, 1905

Chapter 7 – A Lesson Gallery
Society at Large

This dual set of *Brothers* and *Sisters* images were printed on facing pages in the table book *Our Neighbors*.

— AND — SISTERS

Sisters
Our Neighbors, 1905

Lessons From The Gibson Girl
Society at Large

"ON THE SIDEWALKS OF NEW YORK"

On The Sidewalks of New York
Americans, 1900

Chapter 7 – A Lesson Gallery
Society at Large

WAITING FOR BREAD

Waiting for Bread
Americans, 1900

Lessons From The Gibson Girl
Society at Large

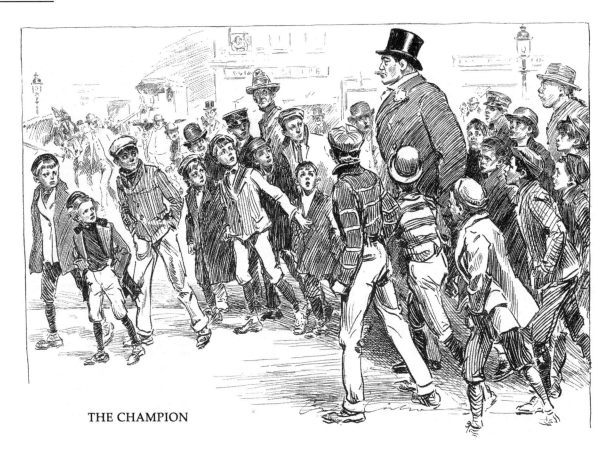

The Champion
Collier's, January 23, 1904

Chapter 7 – A Lesson Gallery
Society at Large

THE CABLE CAR

The Cable Car
Americans, 1900

ON THE FERRY

On The Ferry
Americans, 1900

Lessons From The Gibson Girl
Marital Bliss?

Marital Bliss - Light hearted banter of timeless marriage situations became frequent cartoon subjects.

A Continuous Performance
Life, January 18, 1900

A CONTINUOUS PERFORMANCE

She: IT TELLS HERE OF A MAN IN CHICAGO WHO HASN'T SPOKEN TO HIS WIFE IN FIFTEEN YEARS.

"PERHAPS HE IS WAITING FOR A CHANCE."

Chapter 7 – A Lesson Gallery
Marital Bliss?

Going to See the Doctor...
Life, September 20, 1900

Mrs Dimpleton: I AM GOING TO SEE THE DOCTOR TO-DAY, AND I KNOW HE WILL INSIST UPON MY GOING ABROAD THIS SUMMER.

Dimpleton: NO, HE WON'T. I MET HIM YESTERDAY AND TOLD HIM IF HE SENT YOU ABROAD I COULDN'T PAY HIS BILL.

Lessons From The Gibson Girl
Marital Bliss?

I Don't Think Married Life …
Life, July 15, 1915

"I DON'T THINK MARRIED LIFE IS EVER HAPPY, ANYWAY."
"THEN WHY DON'T YOU DIVORCE YOUR HUSBAND?"
"I'D RATHER QUARREL WITH HIM THAN STRANGERS."

Chapter 7 – A Lesson Gallery
Marital Bliss?

Ice Doesn't Look Very Strong . . .
Life, March 23, 1905

SUGGESTION
WIFE: THE ICE DOESN'T LOOK VERY STRONG, DOES IT?
PERHAPS YOU'D BETTER TRY IT; YOU KNOW YOU WEIGH MORE THAN I DO.

Lessons From The Gibson Girl
Marital Bliss?

The Cook Has Agreed to Stay
Life, April 28, 1904

Mr.: THE COOK HAS AGREED TO STAY.
Mrs: HOW DID YOU MANAGE IT?
"I TOLD HER IT WAS COWARDLY TO LEAVE ME ALONE."

Chapter 7 – A Lesson Gallery
Marital Bliss?

My Wife Tells Me, Sir...
Life, November 19, 1903

"MY WIFE TELLS ME, SIR, THAT YOU HAVE BEEN MAKING LOVE TO HER."

"THAT'S JUST LIKE A WOMAN, TO DISCUSS OUR PRIVATE AFFAIRS. IT WILL BE IN THE PAPERS NEXT."

Lessons From The Gibson Girl
For Love of Mutt

For Love of Mutt – Gibson's favorite animal drawings were of dogs. Some must have been household pets, as the same ones appear frequently.

That's a fine dog . . .
Life, April 30, 1914

"THAT'S A FINE DOG YOU HAVE THERE. WHAT BREED IS IT?"
"SH! NOT SO LOUD! HE *THINKS* HE'S A BULLDOG."

Chapter 7 – A Lesson Gallery
For Love of Mutt

THE FALLEN STAR.
"FOND MEMORY BRINGS THE LIGHT OF OTHER DAYS—."

The Fallen Star
Life, December 2, 1899

Lessons From The Gibson Girl
For Love of Mutt

Refuses To Marry a Nobleman
Life, September 8, 1904

The Education of Mr. Pipp
Life, September 8, 1898

Chapter 7 – A Lesson Gallery
For Love of Mutt

"Now." said Jacqueline, "for my notes. And what are you going to do while I'm busy!" "Watch you, if I may." A smile touched her eyes and lips—a little wistfully. "You know, Mr. Desboro, that I like to waste time with you. Flatter your vanity with that confession. But I must work very hard if I'm every gong to have any leisure in my old age."

The Business of Life
by Robert Chambers
Serialized in *Cosmopolitan*,
February 1913

Lessons From The Gibson Girl
Second Thoughts

Second Thoughts – Gibson drew many cartoons that focused on remorseful decisions, usually involving ill-suited marriages. The *Crooked Tale* cartoon is an uncharacteristic dark piece of work, perhaps it reflected an actual scandalous affair at the time.

A CROOKED TALE
THERE WAS A CROOKED MAN,
WHO MADE A CROOKED DEAL,
AND GOT A CROOKED FORTUNE
BY A VERY CROOKED STEAL,
HE HAD A CROOKED WIFE,
WITH A CROOKED NAME,
AND NOW THEY LIVE APART
IN VERY CROOKED FAME.

A Crooked Tale
Life, May 1, 1902

Chapter 7 – A Lesson Gallery
Second Thoughts

The Lucky Rich
Life, December 31, 1896

Lessons From The Gibson Girl
Second Thoughts

A CASTLE IN THE AIR
THESE YOUNG GIRLS WHO MARRY OLD MILLIONAIRES SHOULD STOP DREAMING.

A Castle in the Air
Collier's, May 30, 1903

Chapter 7 – A Lesson Gallery
Second Thoughts

"ARE YOUR INTENTIONS TOWARD THE WIDOW SERIOUS?"
"OH, VERY. I AM GOING, IF POSSIBLE, TO GET OUT OF MARRYING HER."

Are Your Intentions...
Life, March 3, 1913

Lessons From The Gibson Girl

Career Moves

Career Moves – Gibson drew many different career choices of the new woman, some traditional, some not. Of course all in a humorous vein.

STUDIES IN EXPRESSION
The "chorus girl's" visit home.

The chorus girl's visit home.
Life, October 1, 1903

Chapter 7 – A Lesson Gallery
Career Moves

AND HERE, WINNING NEW FRIENDS AND NOT LOSING THE OLD ONES, WE LEAVE HER.

This cartoon when seen out of context may seem baffling. This was from a long series in 1901 that became a table book titled *A Widow And Her Friends.* The story began when the fictional character became a widow, and depicted the different states of grief, including what to do with herself. Several cartoons dealt with the possibility of becoming a nun.

The cartoon *She Becomes a Trained Nurse* (on the following page) is from the same series.

…Winning New Friends…
Life, July 4, 1901

Lessons From The Gibson Girl
Career Moves

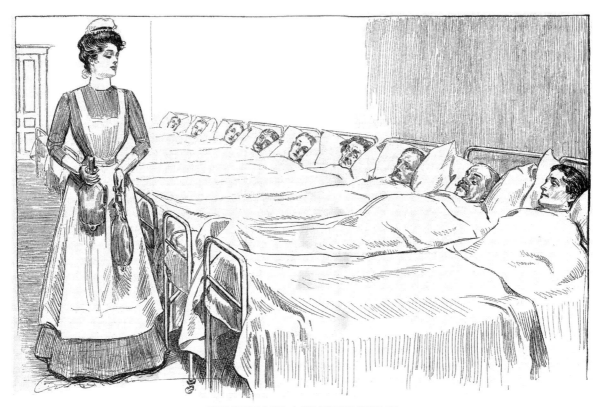

SHE BECOMES A TRAINED NURSE

She Becomes a Trained Nurse.
Life, February 21, 1901

Chapter 7 – A Lesson Gallery
Career Moves

IN DAYS TO COME THE CHURCHES MAY BE FULLER.

In Days To Come...
Life, July 28, 1896

Lessons From The Gibson Girl
On the Edge

On the Edge – Occasionally Gibson drew a sketch or cartoon that may have seemed out of character or touched on controversial topics. However, these examples offer a wonderful look at the emotional range he was capable of depicting.

Chivalry
Life, July 9, 1891

CHIVALRY
Tom Dewitt: WON'T YOU ALLOW ME TO RELIEVE YOU, MISS HOLDER?
Miss Held (indignantly): Sir!
Tom Dewitt: AH, I AM ONLY SOLICITOUS FOR MISS HOLDER. I NEVER COULD BEAR TO SEE A WOMAN DOING A MAN'S WORK.

Chapter 7 – A Lesson Gallery
On the Edge

THE SONG OF THE TROUSSEAU

Wrap, and corset, and gown,
  Sleeve, and ruffle, and band—
Fitting me, up and down—
  As long as I've strength to stand.

Pinning me in and out,
  Basting me out and in,
Vexed that I've grown stout–
  Grumbling because I'm thin.

Watching my eyes and hair,
  Suiting my cheek and neck,
Hauling me here and there,
  Until I'm a perfect wreck.

Band, and ruffle, and sleeve;
  Oh, the first bride was blest–
Dear little happy Eve,
  In Love and innocence dressed

Madeline S. Bridge.

Untitled

Life, April 7, 1892

A wonderful little poem by Madeline S. Bridge laments the toils and trouble of the *dressed* woman. What woman, or man, has not wished to simply discard it all for the freedom of Eve. Gibson's illustration interpreted the poem with perfection.

– 197 –

Lessons From The Gibson Girl
On the Edge

The Salons of New York
At Mrs. Pinckney Johnsons

The Salons of New York
Life, January 26, 1893

In late 1892 and early 1893, Gibson drew a series of cartoons titled *The Salons of New York*. Most were glimpses of social gatherings in well-to-do society houses of notable people.

However, he drew two that were out of the norm, choosing to profile all groups of people in American. One was an African American setting and the other of an informal 'Chowder Club.' Both cartoons received positive comments as they portrayed participants that seemed to actually enjoy the festivities, where the high-society versions showed mostly bored or snooty people trying to impress each other.

At Mrs. Pinckney Johnsons is also notable as minorities were generally not portrayed in positive settings.

Chapter 7 – A Lesson Gallery
On the Edge

THE SALONS OF NEW YORK
AN EVENING WITH THE GENTLEMEN'S SONS CHOWDER CLUB

Gibson must have liked this cartoon, as it was one of thirty-eight drawings he exhibited at the 1893 Columbia Exposition (World's Fair) in Chicago.

Chowder Clubs sprang up all over the country; they were simply informal social clubs of like-minded people. This cartoon appears to be a working class group of people who enjoy dancing and imbibing a little drink.

The Salons of New York
Life, December 15, 1892

Lessons From The Gibson Girl
Domestics

Domestics – The sometimes complex relationship between high society people and their domestic help was frequently a subject of Gibson's wit.

THAT DELICIOUS MOMENT
WHEN YOU ARE SUDDENLY CALLED UPON TO DISCHARGE THE COOK.

That Delicious Moment...
Life, December 3, 1891

Chapter 7 – A Lesson Gallery
Domestics

STUDIES IN EXPRESSION
AN IMITATION OF THE LADY OF THE HOUSE.

An Imitation of the Lady . . .
Life, January 23, 1902

Lessons From The Gibson Girl
Domestics

You Ruined the Terrapin ...
Life, December 22, 1904

Mistress: YOU RUINED THAT TERRAPIN LAST NIGHT, ELLEN. I CAN'T HAVE THINGS WASTED SO.
"SURE, MUM, 'TWASN'T WASTED. WE ATE IT IN THE KITCHEN."

Chapter 7 – A Lesson Gallery
Domestics

STUDIES IN EXPRESSIONS
BRIDGET ANNOUNCES SHE IS ENGAGED TO BE MARRIED.

Bridget Announces She . . .
Life, February 25, 1904

Love Is Everything

Life, August 20, 1891

The man in this drawing looks suspiciously like Gibson himself. Reportedly he self-posed for some cartoons to save modeling fees, especially early in his career.

LOVE IS EVERYTHING.

She: NOW I WANT TO WEAR THE ENGAGEMENT RING AT THE NEXT HOP. PLEASE BE SURE YOU GET IT ON TIME.

He: O THEY HAVE ALREADY TOLD ME THEY WOULD LET ME HAVE IT ON TIME.

Chapter 8

A Real Gibson Girl

Cupid eventually took careful aim at Charles Dana Gibson and ushered both New York's most eligible bachelor and the Gibson Girl into a new dimension. Athletic, handsome, intelligent, and rich – he never flaunted any of it. Humble to a fault, a wise investor, and dedicated to his craft, he was a Boy Scout before there were *Boy Scouts*.

That is not to claim he was a saint, it is just that discretion was respected in his era, and any notable or gossip-worthy affairs are not part of public history.

Gibson was not naive of the world or women, he worked, played, and dined with the most talented and educated people near and far. As noted before, his best friend. R. H. Davis was arguably the *most interesting man in the world*, and Gibson was likely his wingman from New York to London to Paris.

With a lifetime of worldly knowledge accumulated in only twenty-eight years, what kind of woman would capture the heart of C. D. Gibson?

It was his longtime friend and publisher, Robert H. Russell, who maybe knew that answer and introduced Gibson to his future wife, Irene Langhorne. The three of them, Dana, Irene, and the Gibson Girl, all were about to change.

• • •

Southern belles were not merely a myth in the 19th century, they graced Dixie with their own unique style passed down for generations. They came from influential southern families who nearly disappeared during the Civil War, but were resurrected from the war's ashes to help shape the country again.

Irene Langhorne was one of five daughters of Nancy and Chiswell Langhorne from Lynchburg, Virginia. The Langhorne family lost their plantation lands and fortunes during the Civil War, and a young Chiswell turned to jobs as a hotel clerk, livery hand, and auctioneer.[1] Eventually he fashioned a new fortune in the construction business helping to rebuild the South's railroad infrastructure.[2]

The family moved to the rebuilt capital of the Confederate states, Richmond, Virginia where his five pretty daughters were prominent in the social scene. Irene was the second of five girls who all made names for themselves in the upper echelons of society, politics, or business.

As the damaged relationships between the North and South were mending, travel and socializing between the two cultures increased, even eclipsing pre-war levels. Chiswell Langhorne's business success brought him in close contact with northern money centers, where his daughters would join him and spread their charm across Philadelphia, New York, and Washington society.

When a scene called for a singer and a piano, it most likely included Irene.
Sketches and Cartoons, 1898

• • •

Horse shows were popular entertainment and social functions in the 1890s. The automobile was little more than an experiment in a few bicycle shops and was not yet the common mode of transportation or status symbol. Beautiful horses were admired as athletes, and fancy carriages represented the limousine of the day. Gibson drew many cartoons of the pomp and glamour associated with the shows and the elite members of society who went to see and be seen. A *New York Sun* review of a week-long horse show noted:

> *From the point of view of the spectators the show was a success. Those who came there to see society in the boxes saw it. Perhaps it was not as beautiful as imagination had pictured, but still it was society, and it sat their very sleek and docile while was discussed.*

WILD ENTHUSIASM AT THE HORSE SHOW.
DURING A CRITICAL EVENT IN THE RING.

Wild Enthusiasm At…
Life, November 18, 1897

One November 1894 evening, after a show in Madison Square Garden, a dinner was given in honor of Miss Langhorne in the famed Delmonico's restaurant, a favorite haunt of New York's movers and shakers. In one corner of the restaurant, apart from the Langhorne party, sat Robert H. Russell, Richard Harding Davis, and Gibson. Russell, one of Gibson's publishers and a good friend, had met Irene at a formal ball a year before, and promised to introduce her to the dashing duo of Davis and Gibson. Upon Miss Langhorne and her entourage leaving, she passed by Russell who immediately followed her to the door. Returning shortly to Harding and Gibson, Russell announced to his young companions that a *tea* was scheduled for the next day in his apartment to which they were invited to meet the lovely lady.[3]

Whether the timing, encounter, and subsequent tea at Russell's was a coincidence is not known – what is fact is that he set in motion that night a life-changing series of events for Gibson and Irene.

The small social gathering was a success. To use an appropriate word of the time, Gibson was smitten from the little time spent with her at Russell's small gathering. Not one to lose time or to prevent the possibility of some other admirer gaining favor with Irene, he decided he must host his own tea party before she left town for her Richmond home.

Irene was an accomplished pianist and singer, learned perhaps in a southern girls' finishing school. This would be fortuitous for Gibson, not only would he enjoy the pleasure of her talent, but future opportunities to sketch her singing would arise repeatedly.

Gibson's apartment, which doubled as his studio, conveniently sported a grand piano that was a prop for some recent drawings. During the course of his party, someone asked Irene to sing. This may have been the clinching moment for Gibson as his interest would grow beyond mere infatuation. The sketch *A Love Song* is reportedly inspired from that scene as she softly sang *Good-night, Beloved*.

Months of courting and travel to Richmond followed those initial but memorable few days in New York. During visits to the Langhorne home, they went horseback riding many times, away from prying eyes.

Riding across the countryside for exercise of the horses or themselves was probably not their primary interest, as her father offered they " . . . did bring the horses home in good condition, never overtired."[4]

A Love Song.
Life, September 10, 1896
Irene joined by a cupid choir.

After Gibson made a formal request to her father for Irene's hand, the senior Langhorne actually checked his references. The responses must have been acceptable since Irene and Dana's engagement was announced August 14, 1895, ten months after their introduction at Russell's arranged gathering.

• • •

Weddings are meant to be momentous affairs. A lavish one between a prominent southern belle and the world's most famous illustrator would certainly live up to grand expectations.

A private train brought Gibson's friends from New York and Philadelphia to Richmond for the early November ceremony. A society affair with an attentive following, the celebration was generous but not extravagant. A special telegram to the *Philadelphia Times* reported:

> *The excitement and the interest which were everywhere evinced in the marriage culminated in a crowd of colossal proportions that would have filled the sacred edifice many times over.*[5]

Despite the crowds and overwhelming excitement it created in the area, the *Roanoke Times* claimed:

> *The wedding was characterized by the utmost dignity and good taste.*[6]

The guest list included Langhorne connections and Gibson family members from New York and Rhode Island. In addition to expected family, many of the characters of Gibson's drawings played prominent parts in the affair. The best man honor was bestowed upon Dana's brother Langdon. Ushers included Gibson Man and best friend R. H. Davis and fellow model James DeKay. Also in attendance was the infamous matchmaker Robert H. Russell, and John A. Mitchell, Gibson's friend and editor of *Life*.

Gibson Girls were also present. Ethel Barrymore and Helen Benedict, members of a rat pack-like group of Gibson and Harding friends, were on the train. Interestingly, the well known Evelyn Nesbit and her paramour, noted architect Stanford White, were invited guests.

Page One Announcement
Philadelphia Times,
November 8, 1895

Chapter 8 – A Real Gibson Girl

Newlyweds Mr. and Mrs. Charles Dana Gibson saw the world together as they soon left for an extended honeymoon in England and Europe. They enjoyed royal receptions in London and stops in Gibraltar, Spain, Rome, Monte Carlo, and Paris. Not to be mistaken for common tourists, the U.S. Ambassador managed an invitation to Buckingham Palace for the newlyweds, which included an audience with Queen Victoria.[7]

After Presentation (to Queen Victoria) Sketches and Cartoons, 1898

Many sketches on their honeymoon became a table book simply titled *London*. Along with enjoying new doors open to her, Irene understood her husband's art demands, as Downey wrote:

> *There was no wifely protest when on the morning after the honeymooners' arrival in London, the bridegroom peered out of the hotel window, seized pencil and paper and began to sketch a street scene.*[8]

– 211 –

Irene soon became recognized in variety of drawings, independent of playing the artist's wife. One such natural role she fulfilled was that of a singer and pianist for book illustrations. Erroneously, late-comers to the Gibson Girl phenomena believed she was the original Gibson Girl as he drew likenesses of her for twenty years or more.

THEIR PRESENCE OF MIND
THEY HAD BEEN IN THEIR ROOM BUT A MOMENT WHEN THEY WERE STARTLED BY A KNOCK.

Their Presence of Mind
Life, August 8, 1895

This cartoon depicting an awkward newlywed moment was published two months before their wedding. Perhaps Gibson anticipated himself in a likely scenario. The man's overly calm demeanor, bowler and cane lying on the floor, and her disheveled hat and blank stare all indicate guilt of something.

Chapter 8 – A Real Gibson Girl

It was natural that a change soon came to the Gibson Girl. Generally, people mature from the passing of years, changing lifestyles, and added responsibilities. Gibson was maturing, as were his art and characters.

• • •

New parents commonly say bringing a child into the world changed their lives – usually for the better once they catch up on sleep. Dana and Irene became parents of two children within a few years of their wedding. From then forward, his drawings, topics, and satire seemed to take on a kinder and gentler nature.

The Mother
Americans, 1900
Dana and Irene's second child was born in 1899.

That is not to say he lost his bite when crusading for just causes. Between slaying prejudicial dragons or poking fun at the world's ironies he frequently drew the joys of family and children. Sometimes he even mixed the topics with surprising success as this amusing encounter captures how plans can change once children enter the situation.

AFTER FIFTEEN YEARS.
WHEN SHE REFUSED HIM HE VOWED HE WOULD NEVER MARRY.

After Fifteen Years…
Life, April 30, 1903

Whenever Gibson needed a child model he frequently used his younger sisters, particularly Josephine. From the time he and Irene brought their first child into the picture, he began to draw babies, toddlers, and children more often than during his years of bachelorhood. In the sketch *After Fifteen Years*, the children were probably modeled from his family. At the time of the drawing, Dana and Irene's daughter was six years old and their son was four. Not surprising, blessed with marriage and family, Gibson's life and his outlook on the world around him appeared to change from his early days of drawing and commentary.

Indeed, he actually spoke about his own transition in blunt terms during another irritating interview. Ten years into his marriage, a reporter persistently wanted to talk about the Gibson Girl creation. Gibson reacted uncharacteristically when he:

> . . . threw up his hand in an attitude of protest.
>
> 'She is dead, I mean' hastily correcting himself, 'married. And if you have taken the trouble to note, she has quite a family of children . . .' [9]

Even if the press was not ready to move on, C. D. Gibson certainly was.

• • •

Irene possessed a confidence that allowed her to enjoy the couple's frenzied environment and celebrity position in New York. They lived in the center of the city, on the top floor of the *Life* building where she was always near the rush of getting a magazine out once a week. Despite pressures of weekly publishing deadlines and the demands of a full social calendar she handled everything with grace and success. Yet Irene Gibson did not exist solely as the wife of a famous artist, living a life of leisure.

While Dana used his pen to make a positive mark on the world, Irene took an active role in helping the disadvantaged, particularly children. In 1908, Irene along with other notable women founded New York Big Sisters Inc. Their mission as stated in a charities directory was:

> *An association of women individually to take, and secure others to take, a friendly interest in children, especially girls, who have been brought before the Children's Court; and in other children whose physical, mental and moral development has been hindered or endangered because of bad environment or other conditions.*[10]

Mrs. William K. Vanderbilt was president with Mrs. Charles Dana Gibson listed as secretary. Her philanthropy extended to other organizations and causes, especially during the Great War when she helped organize war bond rallies and Red Cross recruiting activities.

The 19th U.S. Constitutional Amendment, granting women full voting rights, was ratified in New York in June 1919 and by December, Irene was involved in founding The Woman's Democratic Club. This organization would help educate and support women in their new role as voters. The club's charter was:

> *Every Democratic woman to do her utmost to strengthen the National Democratic part, but to reserve her individual right to cast her own vote for such measures or candidates as are endorsed by her intellect and ratified by her conscience.*[11]

Seems a sensible way to execute your voting rights - endorse by *intellect* and vote with *conscience* when in conflict with a disagreeable party position or candidate.

• • •

Children were a large part of Irene and Dana's lives; from her early days with aid organizations to their own two children followed by grandchildren. While living in New York, they would escape to family and vacation homes in New England, where their children could experience something other than city madness. Eventually, he would buy an island, appropri-

Irene Gibson (r) with Mabel Choate, noted horticulturist and conservationists. c. 1912

Library of Congress

ately named 700 Acre Island, off the coast of Maine where they retired and his children and their children explored nature as he did when he was a young boy.

Classic image of Irene Langhorne Gibson singing.
Education of Mr. Pipp, 1899

Probably their son Langhorn Gibson, born the same year as the sketch was published.
Education of Mr. Pipp, 1899

Daughter Irene Langhorne Gibson.
Collier's, October 29, 1910

Book cover with Irene. *Sketches in Egypt*, 1898

They lived a fairy tale life, including the "happily ever after" part. Travel to Europe and other exotic locale was common for those who could afford the adventures. They cruised the Mediterranean on a yacht in 1900, visited the Ivory Coast, and experienced the capitals of Western Europe. *McClure's* magazine commissioned a travelogue of Egypt and sent the Gibsons to sketch and write about the ancient land.

While Gibson was a master of words, he was not comfortable writing a book. *Sketches in Egypt*, would be his first and last. As a perfectionist, he found writing difficult, though the book became a delightful read. His revealing drawings of Egypt and its people, along with his honest narrative, educated many people about the mysterious country.

Biographer Downey noted that the book:

> . . . might have come under the general head: The Gibson Girl in Egypt.

She was seen in many drawings, though not in fashionable poses of earlier times. Her casual appearances showed her fascination with the antiquities and wonders of past life in an old civilization. Gibson even placed her on the book's cover.

Irene Langhorne Gibson outlived her husband by twelve years; she passed away in 1956 at the age of 83. Her grace, strength, and character outpaced even the Gibson Girl tag, a lofty bar to clear. She was the perfect and equal partner in life to a man who more than simply imagined the modern woman.

• • •

Chapter 9

Pursuing a Dream

For nearly twenty years, C. D. Gibson ruled the black and white illustration world as the best of his craft. His drawings were unsurpassed and his earning power was the highest in the profession. Yet, Gibson dreamed of becoming an accomplished brush painter in color.

Two decades of creating humorous ink drawings may have become repetitive, his very success trapped him from exploring new horizons. Requests from publishers for his ink sketches perhaps did not interest him, just as some aging rock stars cringe at repetitive requests to sing their hits from previous decades.

Five years into the 20th century it was time for a change. The Gibson Girl deserved more than black and white pen renderings.

Wasting Time
Life, July 19, 1900

Writing for the *New York Times* in the spring of 1905, a reporter conducted a lengthy interview with Gibson for a three-quarter page story. The headline became another trite rendition typical of reporting that Gibson loathed: "Gibson Girl's Creator and American Girl Types." While the interview and subsequent article touched all the worn out reasons of when, how, or why the Gibson Girl was created, buried in the middle were several prophetic responses from Gibson that the reporter failed to seize upon.

> [Gibson] *Of course, some of us can only hope that black and white drawing has come, been seen, and awarded a respectable place in the art world. But it can hardly be claimed by the most presumptuous as of the same high order of art as work in oils, for instance.*
>
> [Reporter] *Have you done anything in oils?*
>
> [Gibson] *Yes. But not for public inspection—yet. I am working constantly in oil, and someday— well, just some day.*[1]

Gibson essentially exposed his inner most thoughts of how he felt about himself, artistic standings, and his future. Yet, the blind reporter continued with simple questions about the models he used and other pedestrian inquiries, while missing a news scoop.

Weekly cartoons were needed to fill magazine pages, and there was not always an interesting crisis or event to cover, or maybe inspiration was lacking within. While his art was always exceptional and drawn with pride, lately some of his work seemed mediocre. In May of 1905, the most stirring cartoon he came up with poked fun at a cross section of women simultaneously adopting *The New Hat* style.

Chapter 9 – Pursuing a Dream

THE NEW HAT

The New Hat
Life, May 18, 1905

For an artist approaching twenty years as the top professional in his field, with personal standards that exceeded any publisher's or reader's, this drawing seemed to fulfill a deadline and not much more.

• • •

Color drawings from fellow artists surrounded Gibson by 1904. *Collier's* was making a big push into color, even though they just signed the largest illustration deal in history for black and white sketches. His friend Frederic Remington was painting in color for many of the same *Collier's* issues that included Gibson sketches, overshadowing the latter's line-art with vivid color renditions of the Wild West. Gibson's black and white genre of line drawings was nearly a generation old. He did experiment in colorizing some line drawings, but this was just a literal cover up.

Color cover art
Life, 1904

Life magazine used color sparingly, possibly because a significant investment in new presses was needed to print what we now think of as full color. By 1902, they printed some issues with spot color, a simple method of overprinting a single color of ink in one spot. The New Year's issue and the Fourth of July issue both featured colorized Gibson drawings on the covers. The portrait featured bright orange/red hair and her lips painted a matching shade of red. The patriotic cover was essentially over printed with three different colors: blue, red, and gold. The coat was navy blue, the trim gold, and the dress included red vertical coloring over white. Both were originally line drawings.

This practice of adding color could not compete with the beauty of a full color print made from a color oil painting with all its subtle nuances. Other artists such as A.B. Frost, J. C. Leyendecker, and Howard Chandler Christy, all who started as line illustrators, garnered recognition and praise in the art world with their color work, especially as the *realism* art movement began to dominate mass produced images. Magazines were increasingly printing more color pages and soon whole issues would be color, which pleased readers, advertisers, and hence publishers.

Leyendecker was a prolific full color illustrator who focused on cover art and high-end advertising. *The Saturday Evening Post* alone published over three hundred covers by Leyendecker. Possibly irritating or making Gibson jealous, Leyendecker's *Vacation* cover for *Collier's* consisted of two lovely women with tennis rackets and golf clubs looking eerily similar to Gibson Girls, yet they were in color. One exhibited a pouty stare at the reader, the other projected a Gibson-like far away gaze. If a reader did not know who the artist was, she might certainly think Gibson was now drawing in color.

Another talented artist, Howard Chandler Christy, drew the most beautiful women in full color. He, as most other color artists, was not interested in satirical sketches like Gibson, but drew purely for artistic creativity, even if much of it was to sell magazines or advertising products. These artists were the forerunners of next-generation painters such as Norman Rockwell who dazzled millions with color homespun scenes that were more life-like than life itself.

The end of the Gibson Girl's reign as an ink cartoon was approaching, which may have been a relief to her creator. Now, maybe he could focus his creative skill on color paintings, something he yearned to do.

• • •

Vacation by J. C. Leyendecker
Collier's, August 7, 1907

Seven months after the aforementioned *Times* interview, front-page headlines shouted Gibson's decision to give up cartoon illustration for serious oil painting studies abroad.

On the first day of December in 1905, newspaper stories covered the news with dull precision, as his plans were actually not secret in the publishing community.

> *Charles Dana Gibson, the artist, sailed for Europe on the White Star liner Republic yesterday afternoon. He goes away for a long time to study painting in oils. Mr. Gibson was accompanied by his family, and after landing in Italy will proceed to Madrid.*[2]

On departure, Gibson offered an explanation to reporters, though he had been showered with going away parties and well wishes for some time and the story was oft repeated by now.

> *"I am not going away for good," said Mr. Gibson. "We are going to Madrid and if I get well located it may be two years before we return. My object, of course, you know, is to study painting in oil. I will not say that I have entirely given up my black and white work, for such is not my present intention. I will say, however, that I am going to do nothing along that line for some time.*[3]

Though he was still under contract with *Collier's* for the balance of one hundred drawings negotiated some two years earlier, discussions must have given *Collier's* some comfort their deal would still be advantageous. One day after their celebrity artist sailed for Europe, the magazine ran a notice in the *New York Times* stating:

> *Charles Dana Gibson will work henceforward only in color. By special arrangement, all of his work sent from abroad for reproduction will appear exclusively in Collier's.*[4]

While his fans, and probably some business partners, were stunned by his decision, no animosity was evident from any quarter.

Embodying a festive spirit, one of his finest send-offs was a drawing by fellow artist Victor Perard of a fanciful collage of many Gibson characters bidding *Au Revoir* from the pier.

AU REVOIR

Au Revoir by Victor Perard
Life, November 30, 1905

One year in Spain, one in Paris, and a final year in Italy was the grand plan to become a master artist in oil – or at least a better one. Gibson had invested his money well, or his advisors had. He realized as an artist that financial expertise was not his specialty, and left his wealth management in the hands of trusted professionals. Though his income would drop precipitously, royalties from prints, books, and other products would still contribute to his funds.

Still, many in the world were astonished that he was leaving a yearly income of $65,000 to simply learn how to paint. That sum sounds not so huge today, merely the price of a very nice car or maybe a down payment on a house. In 1905 however, it held the buying power of at least $1.8 million in today's value. He really wanted to learn how to paint.

Gibson forwarded a few drawings to his publishers in New York while in Europe that revealed his work with new techniques and use of color. Artists throughout Europe were exploring radically new directions that included Art Nouveau, modernism, and soon the extreme cubism of Picasso and others.

Cover drawing with European influence, drawn while in Spain.

Life, Christmas Issue, 1906

Gibson experimented with elements of new art movements, though he did not stray far from classical styles. While studying in Spain, he drew the 1906 Christmas cover art for *Life*, a noticeable change from any previous work. This may have been a message of "Hey America, look what I'm doing." It was not an oil painting, but was different from his staid black and white line drawings and a noticeable deviation from his Victorian roots, including the use of geometric elements in the titles.

The year in Madrid complete, he moved as planned to one of his favorite cities, Paris. It had been twenty years since his first trip, and the lapse in time was evident as his stay would be considerably different from his previous Bohemian experience. Still quite familiar with the city after his many visits, he probably enjoyed showing Irene and his children, now ten and eight years old, around the City of Lights.

His desire to study painting in Europe was progressing as planned. The children were experiencing a variety of cultures and wonders of the old world. The family was on a care-free course as they sailed through life.

• • •

Chapter 9 – Pursuing a Dream

The 'Panic of 1907' struck the stock market and financial institutions while Gibson was in Paris, including the Knickerbocker Trust Company where many of Gibson's investments were placed. The country was already in a recession, and massive panic-driven bank withdrawals were common. Gibson's finances were severely damaged, halting his well-planned journey to become an accomplished oil painter while having no worry of supporting his family.

Banks and financial institutions have repeatedly gambled on opportunities to reap huge profits, usually from risky ventures. This practice has repeated itself throughout history, dotting financial history as regular as tide and moon phases.

That 1907 collapse has a familiar ring to a number of market crashes from the Great Depression to the 'sub-prime' financial debacle of 2008. Investment moguls and many politicians had short memories, and many today seem plagued with the same affliction.

The *Some Ticker Faces* cartoon captured mesmerized investors and traders of all ages *then*. One can image the same Wall Street scenario playing out *now* in front of a computer monitor or portable device.

• • •

SOME TICKER FACES

Some Ticker Faces
Collier's, January 16, 1904

Studies with the Europe's finest art masters were cut short. Italian influence would not mold his brush strokes, as Paris saw him bid *au revior* and return to America. Plans for a life of painting in oil would be delayed as he felt the need to rebuild financial security for his family once more. Black and white illustration could still command handsome payment – C. D. Gibson was the master at this medium.

Stepping back into the same situation he left two years earlier was not a simple move. The commercial illustration business was noticeably evolving to different styles and mediums, driven by progressive artists. Color realism artwork from Remington, Christy, Harrison, and others was popular and in high demand.

The flapper, progressive ideas, a world war, and national suffrage were on the nation's horizon. However, Gibson was not a defeatist. America was changing; he, his art, and the Gibson Girl would change with it.

The Sweetest Story Ever Told
Collier's, August 13, 1910

"The Sweetest Story Ever Told"

Chapter 10

Noir et Blanc

Gibson returned from Europe in the spring of 1908, ironically this was nearly twenty years after his initial studies in Paris. Abandoning color, he once again became captive to *noir et blanc* – black and white.

He kept a low profile until the fall, possibly contemplating career and life options. *Collier's* still held the contract for one hundred drawings signed before the sabbatical, and wished to continue publishing his work. They proudly proclaimed their star's return on the December 5th cover, showcasing his leading lady.

Cover Artwork
Collier's, December 5, 1908

However, still not ready to resume drawing society satire, *Collier's* convinced him to try a new genre of subjects, and sent him on a tour of the western United States.

As soon as this project was announced, a *New York Times* reporter penned the headline "C. D. Gibson Returns to Black and White" over a gloomy story about Gibson's state of mind and future. Declaring the artist's past efforts dead and his recent attempts at oil painting a failure, he based the article on hearsay and unidentified comments, never quoting Gibson himself.

Addressing the upcoming trip out West, the reporter set about predicting Gibson's prospects,

> . . . *the insolent, half-closed lids of the society beauty [Gibson Girl] and the square-jawed type of society man will become a thing of the past and in their place will appear big men of the west and characters drawn from every sphere of life the country over.*[1]

The westward journey did not produce a new block buster direction for the artist whose forte was capturing the personality of New York, London, and Paris. He would not draw Indians, calvary soldiers, and cattle drives like his friend Frederic Remington.

Gibson returned to the streets of New York in 1909 and quickly published at least ten drawings in Collier's, the majority being prime double-pages, though nary a scruffy mountain man appeared. These illustrations were not retro versions of the Gibson Girl, but included a variety of more mature women along with a few cartoons focused on lingering social issues.

It appeared C. D. Gibson was trying to find his way, with new and old styles, back into the business of drawing for other people.

Chapter 10 – Noir et Blanc

No Time for Politics
Collier's, August 21, 1909

Throughout his career, Gibson appeared to draw from his heart. *No Time for Politics*, probably a portrait of his wife and daughter, seemed to reflect a change of priorities in his life, which along with the caption conveys not only a disdain for politics of the governmental sort, but possibly business, finance, and other worldly irritations. A familiar frustration even in the 21st century.

• • •

The lead male character in *The Common Law*, by Robert W. Chambers, 1911

Illustration by C. D. Gibson

Bigger changes were coming Gibson's way as he eased back into the magazine illustration routine. They were not as motivating as his desire for oil studies, but they would come to be very lucrative while reuniting him with old friends.

Cosmopolitan's art editor, who Gibson knew from his earliest professional days, offered him an assignment to illustrate a book for even an older friend, Robert W. Chambers. Chambers had sat next to Gibson in the New York art school in 1883, but instead of pursuing an artist's life, he became a best-selling author. *Cosmopolitan* was preparing to publish Chamber's new book in eight installments, and the publisher wanted Gibson to illustrate the story – six panels for each installment. According to Gibson's biographer Fairfax Downey ". . . the assignment did not appeal to him." However, he was pleased to be asked by such a respected man and was just as pleased with the $900 per installment.[2]

Chamber's book, *Common Law*, became a best seller and the serialized version increased *Cosmopolitan's* circulation dramatically. Downey characterized the book as "the sex-thriller of the day," a genre that has continually proved popular. Indeed, when word of nude scenes in the book leaked out, readers scrambled to find the passages to see if Gibson drew them as written. Sadly, they were disappointed at this omission. However, the readers were not disappointed with the sultry illustrations that added heat to the story. Both the leading woman and leading man were in today's vernacular, hot, maybe even *smoking hot!*

The Common Law,
by Robert W. Chambers, 1911
Illustration by C. D. Gibson

From a steamy scene just thirty pages into the book, the young model is concerned that having lunch with the artist was not proper as they broke from painting a nude scene:

> "I know perfectly that this isn't right," she said, helping him and then herself. "But I am wondering what there is about it that isn't right."[3]

Cosmopolitan took a page out of *Collier's* playbook by engaging *the highest-paid illustrator and the highest-paid novelist*.[4] It worked. *Cosmopolitan's* readership more than quadrupled. The magazine itself proclaimed:

> The Chambers-Gibson combination is unquestionably the biggest hit of the decade in the magazine world . . .[5]

The Chambers and Gibson team worked so well, *Cosmopolitan* secured the duo for no less than six more books, and engaged Gibson to illustrate additional projects.

In addition to the *Cosmopolitan* assignments, and the exclusive *Collier's* agreement aside, Gibson was in demand by *Good Housekeeping*, *McCall's*, *McClure's*, and the *International*. Drawings for these publications were generally more sophisticated than his prior magazine work and included color treatment of covers. While these were not traditional oil works, they showed a new and pleasant side of his artistic talent. Color came to the Gibson Girl.

Color magazine covers by Gibson.
Cosmopolitan, February, 1911
McClure's, November, 1912

• • •

While Gibson was in Europe, *Life* magazine found artists to replace his black and white drawings, one was a talented artist that was Gibson understudy for several years. Ten years younger that Gibson, R.M. Crosby drew many secondary sketches for *Life* when Gibson was the lead illustrator.

His style and humor closely resembled Gibson's work and it earned him plenty of cover assignments and double-page spreads while Gibson was in Europe. The May 6, 1909 cover with a sportsman theme looked eerily like a Gibson drawing in style, content and humor.

Crouched in a blind on the water's edge, a woman duck hunter sits with cupid and waits for the waterfowl to descend before firing. The bobbing wooden decoys were carved as little men with top hats and coats. As the birds descend, they appear as unsuspecting men. How Gibson-like.

Gibson-like art by R. M. Crosby. *Life*, May 6, 1909

Several years passed before Gibson rejoined *Life* on a regular basis. A few drawings appeared in 1912 and gradually grew to more than fifty in 1915. *Life* magazine was still in his veins and in a few years it would become a major focus of his being again.

Until then his creativity seemed to lack focus and passion, though occasionally a poignant cartoon stirred one's thought. Perhaps he was reflecting on the financial calamity that placed him in this position as he chastised investors to "Go Down To The Street" and possibly see the real world.

Advice To The Mentally Feeble
Life, February 6, 1913

ADVICE TO THE MENTALLY FEEBLE
GO DOWN TO THE STREET

Except for an occasional gem, his cartoons seemed to suffer from an artist's version of 'writer's block.' Most of his book assignments were complete by 1914 and magazine projects that he previously dominated were captured by younger artists who drew newer fashions with attitude. Nothing seemed to motivate the fifty-year-old artist – for now.

• • •

The World was about to change – the entire world. Travel to Europe was extremely popular around the turn of the century. Different reasons drove people to endure a week-long Atlantic crossing, though many simply enjoyed the comfort and pampering provided by luxury liners. Others went for adventure and exploration of foreign cultures. Some sought high society, royalty, and stature, some studied and learned from masters in art or the sciences.

The result was that many Americans gained a true fondness for England and the continental countries of Europe – including their people. Gibson was one who felt a kinship with the English and the French. They both influenced his art and himself as a man, and he took any grievous threat to them personally.

The horrors of an impending global war caught the United States woefully unprepared, both militarily and in conscience. The Great War, a term soon to be a daily utterance, started as regional political chaos then catastrophically boiled over, scorching most of Europe and singeing much of the rest of the world, including the United States.

Few understood the turmoil in Europe. Many believed any disturbance was purely local, it would run its course, and certainly not impact America. All were misguided and wrong.

"IT'S AN ILL WIND THAT BLOWS NOBODY ANY GOOD."

It's An Ill Wind . . .
Life, March 11, 1897

The ". . . Ill Wind . . ." drawing was published during the run-up to the Spanish-American War, a time when the United States was wrestling with intervening in support of Cuba's fight for independence from Spain.

He recognized that war was never a good option, only one of last resort. Yet, if it was inevitable or the only solution to a worse scenario, he would not shy from his duty, and even enlist the Gibson Girl to help fight for freedom and justice.

• • •

Chapter 11

Gibson Girl Goes to War

The Great War inflicted millions of casualties on France, England, and other allies before the U. S. entered the war in April 1917. For thirty-two previous months, American sentiment ranged from outrage to isolationism to pacifism, as reluctance to help our friends and allies sadly dominated official policy.

Charles Dana Gibson was part of the outrage and enlisted the Gibson Girl as his chief messenger to confront the United States' enemies.

A GIRL IN TIPPERARY
"My Heart's Right There"

A Girl in Tipperary
Life, December 3, 1914

The sketch of a tearful woman reading war reports includes a caption that referenced what would become the most popular English war song, *It's a Long Way to Tipperary*.

• • •

A year before Congress declared war, Gibson was already firing his pen at the Kaiser, the German military machine, and German associates known as the Central Powers.

Falling political dominos triggered the war in 1914. First was the assassination of Archduke Franz Ferdinand, heir to the throne of the Austro-Hungarian Empire, by Serbian rebels. In turn the empire declared war on Serbia. Russia, an ally of Serbia, then declared war on Austria-Hungary. Germany, in allegiance to Austria-Hungary, turned on Russia. Germany further declared war on France and neutral Belgium, causing England to enter the war in support of France.

Historians have debated various motives for the war including one suggestion that power-hungry German military leaders instigated most of the aggression, over the will of their own people. Many of Gibson's illustrations reflected that idea as he felt empathy for innocent German civilians.

The *Great War*, as it was called before we started numbering world wars, did not officially see the United States enter until April of 1917. Astonishingly, this was nearly two years after the English passenger liner RMS Lusitania was sunk by German U-boats, killing 1,198 passengers and crew, including 128 Americans.

Ambivalence towards joining the war pervaded the thoughts of politicians in Washington, while German aerial bombardment of England raged in early 1915.

• • •

Since the early days of avoiding political cartoons in *Tid-Bits*, Gibson shunned controversial political topics throughout most of his career. However, *Life* magazine's position on the war was clear. John Mitchell, *Life's* owner and editor, was emotionally tied to France from the years he spent in Paris as a architectural student. He wrote scathing editorials and commissioned many illustrations that chastised the U.S. *laissez-faire* or hands-off, policy towards the war.

The February 10, 1916 *Life* issue was devoted to the war discussion, with a shocking map of the United States redrawn to reflect a German-led victory. Mitchell's cover was ominous, warning of a possible future.

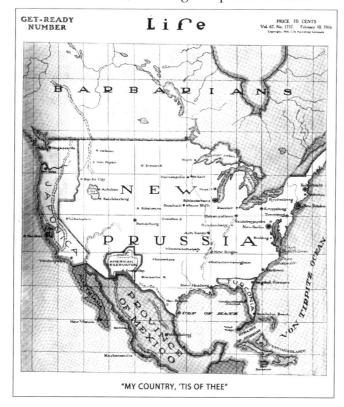

My Country, 'Tis of Thee
Life cover, February 10, 1916

Gibson began his all-out assault on the German-led enemy around the first anniversary of the May 1915 Lusitania sinking. Perhaps the aggressive stance of *Life* editor John A. Mitchell spurred him to join the battle, or the series of dreadful turns in the war convinced him that action was needed. One of the worst battles of the war was underway, The Battle of Verdun, which inflicted one million casualties. The Germans were about to resume unrestricted submarine warfare, discarding an agreement negotiated after the Lusitania sinking. The war was not going to be short or end without U.S. involvement.

Denial was the word of the year in 1916. Congress and President Wilson refused to believe Germany posed a threat, while Germany denied it was responsible for atrocities in Europe or was less than a friend to America. Refuting these falsehoods was left to newspaper and magazine editorials and cartoons across the country. Gibson did not buy the German's rhetoric and addressed this very problem in the April 1916 issue of *Life*, his first cover in nine years.

How Long Will She Stand It?

With a blood-stained tunic, the German Kaiser is testing the limit of Columbia's patience.

Life, April 27, 1916

HOW LONG WILL SHE STAND IT?

Germany recognized that the U.S. was reluctant to get involved in the war, and used this hesitancy as an advantage in a number of ways. False promises to cease submarine warfare, denying they would keep conquered territories, and claiming they were not a threat to the North American were just some of the lies they brazenly spread.

He even chastised Uncle Sam who represented the inept Washington decision makers, as Congress refused to fund military defenses, leaving the country with a small ill-equipped army and an aging fleet.

• • •

A War in Europe!
Life, June 15, 1916

"WELL, WELL! BLESS MY SOUL! IF THERE ISN'T A WAR IN EUROPE!"

Gibson Girls in wartime settings were depicted as everything that was virtuous, right and strong about humanity. Their garments, headbands, or belts were frequently labeled *Columbia*, *Democracy*, *Liberty*, or other honorable traits. They were strong, resilient, and even capable of delivering a deathblow to the enemy, while showing compassion and care for wounded soldiers and innocent victims.

Gibson once again became *Life's* most prolific illustrator, capturing covers and double-page drawings again with a barrage of war-related themes. The next few years his drawings were found in nearly every issue of the magazine, with the majority focused on war atrocities. Gibson and *Life* were on the forefront of bringing a reality to the citizens of the United States. More than creating mere entertainment, Gibson now crossed into territory he avoided for twenty-five years, that of a serious editorial cartoonist.

The German propaganda machine continued attempts to fool America with lies, deceit, and cover-ups through early 1917, though the Gibson Girl continued to remind America that the Kaiser could not be trusted.

Let Me See Your Hands
Life, September 7, 1916

"LET ME SEE YOUR HANDS"

His Word of Honor?
Life, January 18, 1917

His Word of Honor?

Spring is normally a joyous and celebrated time for all things new and bright, though such was not the case in 1917. Germany resumed unrestricted submarine warfare off the coast of North America while expanding raids on South American shipping to England and France.

Still, the tipping point of United States opinion was not realized until the interception and subsequent translation of a telegram from the German Secretary of State to Mexico with a proposal for Mexico to join Germany and declare war on the United States. The proposal included an enticement that Mexico could reclaim territories in New Mexico, Arizona, and Texas.[1] This was a bold, though faulty move by Germany.

Stop the Show
Life, March 8, 1917
Appeared seven days after release of the German telegram to Mexico.

"STOP THE SHOW"

Gibson's drawings were no longer subtle jabs at political leaders and idle threats to the Central Powers. His drawings were forceful and clear.

Congress finally issued a *Declaration of War* in April 1917 after sitting on the sidelines for three years and one month after the telegram

The first issue of *Life* after the declaration featured Gibson's stylized idea of Lady Liberty leading Uncle Sam charging up the hill carrying the U.S. colors as cowering German soldiers retreat.

For Humanity, Cover Art
Life, April 19, 1917

FOR HUMANITY

• • •

Approaching his fiftieth birthday, C. D. Gibson was past the age of active military service, yet he answered the call to duty by leading an army of illustrators. He was not alone in his desire to help the U.S. war effort, contributions from his peers in the art and publishing community quickly became posters the moved a country.

The Society of Illustrators was founded in 1901 as a social and professional organization to bring like-minded artists together. Not surprising, Gibson was society president from 1904 to 1907, and then from 1909 to 1921,[2] his leadership skills were indisputable.

Many artists in the society had drawn cartoons condemning the Central Powers and supporting England, France, and Belgium. Patriotism ran high among them. Within two weeks of the declaration of war, a society meeting was called to discuss how their collective efforts could contribute to U. S. goals. As might be expected in any gathering of successful people, there was bickering and disagreement about what to do and how to proceed. Ironically, the answer would come in the middle of the fray as if it was ordained.

Gibson received a telegram during the meeting from George Creel, the newly appointed Chairman of the Committee on Public Information in the War Department. Creel was an ex-newspaperman and was quite familiar with Gibson's skills and leadership standing – and of course his position on the war through recent illustrations.

Instantly, this telegram gave the society direction. The telegram asked Gibson to:

> . . . *appoint a committee to help in producing whatever artwork the government would need . . . and accept the position of Chairman of the Division of Pictorial Publicity.*[3]

No better qualified and devoted person could have been chosen.

This was an unpaid job in a newly created War Department group, which coincidentally was the same payment hundreds of volunteer artists insisted upon: none. Over the course of the war, they created thousands of posters on every topic the government could think of to help recruit service people and motivate America in the war effort. A story in the *New York Times Magazine* headlined:

> ***The artists of the nation have banded together under the leadership of Charles Dana Gibson to help win the war with brush and pen.***[4]

Gibson appointed various vice-chairmen, perhaps the most important was *Collier's* art director Frank Casey who *knew every artist in town*.[5] Casey's job was to assign specific artists to projects that best suited them as the poster themes were quite diverse.

National League for Woman's Service by C. D. Gibson
Library of Congress

Beautiful posters were created for the Red Cross, Board of Food Administration, American Field Service (ambulance and medical services), Liberty Bonds, American Library Association (collected books for soldiers), YMCA and YWCA, countless charities, and of course the Army, Navy, and Merchant Marine.

Gibson drew fewer posters than some of the best artists since his role as leader and motivator for the group, along with coordinating the many government agencies were enormous tasks and responsibilities themselves. However, the posters he did draw became icons of the era. In addition, during the war years he produced over one hundred drawings for *Life* magazine, many of them poster quality.

A touching Navy recruiting poster showing a proud yet concerned mother offering her young son for service became one of C. D. Gibson's most memorable drawings of all time. Gibson's inspirational Uncle Sam resembled a chiseled Abraham Lincoln and his son Langhorne posed as the handsome young man.

Here he is, Sir.
Navy recruiting poster.
The sketch also appeared in
Life, April 19, 1917
Library of Congress

Managing the poster campaign for the Department of Pictorial Publicity was Gibson's second job, though it may have been first in his heart. He still was a lead illustrator for *Life* magazine, placing near-weekly editorial drawings in the publication.

Yet, the magazine provided a different outlet for his sharpest wit and even outrage. He believed fellow artists should create posters . . . *that would cause the same emotions as are felt when one sees a Belgian child dying for want of food* . . .[6] These motivating works of art are different than cartoons that are more political or angry in nature. Hence, any proposed posters were scrutinized for maximum effect on the American citizens. Posters were subject to approval by the War Department, where any overly critical images of the war effort probably did not pass muster. Casey travelled weekly from New York to Washington with up to seventy-five pounds of drawings seeking approval.

His work for *Life* allowed Gibson to continue with patented critiques of those who deserved them. When war was declared on the Central Powers, the United States possessed the smallest land army of any major power, ships were out of date, as was the horse-drawn field artillery and equipment. Planning and logistics had been ignored, as Lady Columbia reminded Uncle Sam by pointing to PREPARATION on an eye chart.

Fortified by his life-long intensive work habits, Gibson still drew searing cartoons for *Life* while effectively managing the poster campaign. Biographer Fairfax Downey noted in Gibson's biography,

> *This war had moved him as politics never had been able to do.*[7]

Now Then, The Last Line.
Pointing to 'PREPARATION'
Life, May 18, 1917

"NOW THEN, THE LAST LINE"

Other artists drew equally well if not great. Perhaps the most famous poster of the era, since it is still used today and is reincarnated in infinite versions, is the *I Want You* drawing by James Montgomery Flagg. A prolific artist and a contemporary of Gibson, Flagg actually used himself as the model for what would become the most recognized version of Uncle Sam throughout U.S. history. Only forty-years-old at the time, Flagg employed a little artistic creativity in the depiction, as his own face was not quite that chiseled.

James Montgomery Flagg
Library of Congress

I Want You poster for the Division of Pictorial Publicity, Department of War, 1917
by James Montgomery Flagg
Library of Congress

Lessons From The Gibson Girl

It is not surprising that Gibson used his ability to evoke emotion in posters such as *Men Wanted* where a military man's *hero* status attracted admiration from the opposite sex.

THE GIRL HE LEFT BEHIND HIM   MEN WANTED

The Girl He Left Behind Him
Life, November 22, 1917

Men Wanted
Life, July 26, 1917

The call for service was not limited to men and women for military duty, but also for conservation of goods and resources by each American citizen. Much of the poster work and Gibson's cartoons focused on the homeland.

War preparedness and support affected every family in the country whether they contributed sons to the fighting effort or saved resources to feed and equip the military. The Red Cross went from a small service organization to a worldwide army of nurses, doctors, and ambulance drivers. Their activities in the United States included recruitment rallies and fund raisers to support the overseas efforts and even to train children in first aid to relieve a shortage of medical professionals in the U.S.

Gibson's Red Cross drawings covered heroic images and appalling ones that elicited anger towards the enemy. One particularly gruesome illustration revealed a side of Gibson that most readers would not have believed existed. Two Prussian soldiers standing over the body of a fallen nurse may have been his most unexpected and shocking cartoon.

CONGRATULATIONS OF PRUSSIAN SPORTSMEN

Congratulations of Prussian Sportsmen
Life, December 20, 1917

Always the master of motivation, he inspired the reader with powerful and proud messages such as a symbolic battlefield nurse. For those who doubt Gibson's depth of artistic character by only viewing playful Gibson Girl drawings, a quick study of his wartime illustrations may instill a profound appreciation of a more complex artist.

The Red Cross
Life, August 2, 1917

Another year and scores of illustrations would eventually bring an end to Gibson's war duties. Defeat overcame the German military machine when their sailors mutinied in October of 1918 in the face of an inevitable outcome. A month later, the Kaiser abdicated and a few days later, an armistice was signed.

While the United States was officially in the war only twenty months, the conflict had taken a four-year toll. The obvious joy was that the killing stopped and the young men and women would come home.

Gibson drew nearly two hundred war-related cartoons and posters for *Life* and the War Department, representing every facet and emotion that war wrings from human beings.

The Division of Pictorial Publicity submitted *seven hundred poster designs to fifty-eight separate government departments and patriotic committees.*[8]

A Division *victory* dinner honored the artists and particularly Gibson. Architect Cass Gilbert paid tribute:

> *No one else could have done what he did. The great character of the man, rising above all personal considerations, shone forth in his intense earnestness and patriotic fervor; he molded the divergent views of the active minds around him into one composite impulse of service . . .*[9]

The Great War gave the country many heroes and leaders; men and women who put aside personal goals to rally the country into one cohesive force. The Gibson Girl appealed to and rallied the young and old, mothers and fathers, and of course those who met the enemy directly. She portrayed fierce strength and compassion. Sacrifice and bravery. Resolve and hope. All things American.

• • •

War Poster Artists to Hold Victory Banquet

Artists of America who contributed patriotic posters to the Allied cause are to celebrate their share in the victory tonight with a dinner and dance at the Hotel Commodore. It is expected that more than 3,000 person will attend the function.

The dinner is in reality a testimonal to Charles Dana Gibson, head of the division of pictorial publicity of the Committee on Public Information, but he will not know it until he takes his place in the toastmaster's seat. As a matter of fact, Mr. Gibson has been the chief organizer of the dinner, and now it is to be utilized by his friends as a gathering in his honor.

James Fraser, the sculptor, will present a life-size bust he made of Mr. Gibson to the artist, and there are other surprises in store for him. The souvenirs for the guests will be an artistic record of the help of the artists in winning the war.

New York Tribune
February 13, 1919

Lessons From The Gibson Girl

He's Coming Back
Life, December 5, 1918

"HE'S COMING BACK"

Chapter 12

Life Moves On

Life suffered its own casualty during the Great War. Though they did call him the *General,* and no one was more fervent in the quest to defeat the German onslaught, he was not a military man. John Ames Mitchell, founder, majority owner, editor, mentor, indeed the heart and soul of *Life*, died in June of 1918. The timing was cruel as he did not live to see victory over the Kaiser and Central Powers, a battle he fought well before it was a popular position.

It was Mitchell who purchased a Gibson drawing in 1886. It was Mitchell who was Gibson's mentor for over thirty years. It was Mitchell who brought business acumen to Gibson and helped make the artist rich beyond the imagination of a young boy cutting out animal silhouettes for sale to a milkman.

The General was an architect, artist, and writer who possessed exceptional talents that usually escapes people of artistic bent – he was a marketing genius, exceptional manager of people, and effective chief executive.

As the senior editor holding sway over one of the most popular magazines in the world, he could command young artists to shake in their shoes if he chose. Graciously, that was not his style, he strove to nurture new talent. Gibson became a testament to that.

TO SEE THE ART EDITOR

To See the Art Editor

Perhaps how Gibson saw the wait for an audience with John A. Mitchell

Collier's, November 18, 1895

A marketing visionary, he recognized how *Life's* artwork, primarily that from Gibson's pen, could reach fans in ways beyond the weekly printed page – they were willing to pay for images reprinted or applied to any number of products. However, more than treating his readers simply as sources of revenue, Mitchell engaged them in ways similar to social media strategies today, he gave them a voice.

Life frequently ran contests where an untitled Gibson Girl cartoon appeared in the magazine, and readers were asked to submit the caption for prizes up to $500. Usually the top ten finalists were published in subsequent issues, along with submitter's names for their fifteen minutes of fame. Other contests asked readers to identify different Gibson Girls or other characters from the past. This type of customer interaction is not unlike submitting comments to a blog, replying to a Facebook post, or bantering back and forth on Twitter. Mitchell was one hundred years ahead of the world by using social media of the time to increase readership.

Even though he was seventy-three years of age at his death, no transition had been planned or successor chosen for the continuation of *Life*. He would live forever – perhaps that was his one failing. The other co-founder and twenty-five percent owner was Secretary-Treasurer Andrew Miller, a great behind-the-scenes business manager but without the dynamic leadership of Mitchell. Even if he could have stepped in with equal management ability, Miller himself died eighteen months later. Who would run *Life*?

• • •

Mitchell's heirs, owning seventy-five percent of *Life*, put the magazine up for sale shortly after his death. There was still great interest in the business, and it attracted prominent investors and industry giants. Doubleday publishing was becoming a dominate player in the magazine business, itself arising out of *McClure's*. Several long-tenured employees of *Life*, with Gibson as their new patriarch, did not want to see the company sold to an impassioned corporation – so they bought it. A syndicate led by Gibson outbid Doubleday for controlling interest in *Life*. Gibson and the new investors took over *Life* on April 1, 1920. The purported sale price was $900,000, roughly equivalent to $10,000,000 in 2016.

Announcement of *Life* purchase by Gibson and others.
Brooklyn Daily Eagle, March 22, 1920

GIBSON BUYS "LIFE"

Charles Dana Gibson, the artist, has purchased from the widow of John A. Mitchell the controlling interest in Life, the humorous weekly. He will take active charge of the publication on April 1. G. B. Richardson and George Utassy, it was announced, will be associated with him. It was to Life that Mr. Gibson at the age of 18 sold his first pen and ink drawing for $4.

The employee takeover was as much an emotional commitment as a financial and business plan. Both founders, who were active on a day-to-day basis, were now dead within eighteen months of each other. While current employees would take over the executive and management leadership, though the successors were not as skilled at business as the two men who made *Life* a success for over thirty-five years.

Mitchell's life-long business style was congenial, while firmly managing a gaggle of personalities. He was likable, but did not try to be 'mister nice guy.' Gibson tried to appease too many of his coworkers who now were also investors. He listened too much and did not decide enough. Downey noted that after Mitchell died:

Life changed from an absolute monarchy to a democracy governed by a president, vexed by an unruly cabinet and congress.[3]

A look at the new *Life* masthead revealed a warning of the new regime by committee. Before Mitchell died, the masthead simply listed him as President and Miller as Secretary-Treasurer. Now, the multitude of important people increased to seven, too many voices for efficient company management.

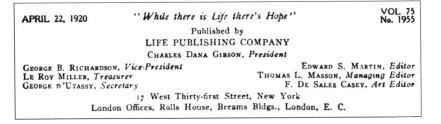

Life masthead with expanded management.

Life, April 22, 1920

Chapter 12 – Life Moves On

Great changes in the United States followed the Great War. In addition to seeing the last vestiges of Victorian style fading away, moral, political, and social foundations evolved at a pace never experienced before. Women's suffrage, post-war industrialization, media changes, and personal consumption habits affected everyday life and businesses.

Fighting the Great War actually gave *Life*, Gibson, and the Gibson Girl an extension of popularity and success. At age fifty, Gibson was not in tune with the current styles, fashion, nor the morals of the pre-flapper era. Victorian dress, attitude, and decorum had given way to a more sassy style by 1915. Corsets were discarded for sleek straight-line dress forms. Easily maintained *bobbed* hair was replacing the swooping chignon hairstyles that required much fussing. "The female form had been planed down to a boyish silhouette."[1] Beyond those images, women were smoking in public, drinking like boisterous men, and dancing in gyrations unseen just ten years before.

Gibson did not easily take to drawing the new vogue, perhaps this contributed to him not rejoining the *Life* team before the war. He also was not in touch with the new readership. As he aged, so did his characters. His men and women were no longer young and frivolous, but mature and respected. His biographer, Fairfax Downey reflected on Gibson's attempt at drawing the flapper:

> *When Gibson's pen outlined her, there was apparent more than a trace of the wonder, the incomprehension, and the dismay of the older generation beholding a rather alarming phenomenon.*[2]

The war actually put many *new-age* changes on hold as everyone's focus was on the nation's troubles. Threatening world affairs distracted the young from flaunting new life-styles and prevented the old from noticing. The bold images of *Columbia* and her sisters confronting

Gibson's view of the '20s style.
Life, February 26, 1920

German soldiers nudged flappers from top billing. The young women with bobbed hair and slinky dresses would have to wait to takeover.

To readers born after 1900, *Life* was their mothers' magazine. Nothing wrong with those mothers or their tastes, but the younger set was not buying the same styles and values. Publications depend on new subscribers as older ones drop off for any number of reasons, and if they are not replaced a magazine's future is in jeopardy.

While Gibson's drawings were not controversial or necessarily brain busters, they were still occasionally cute. However, the slightly touching 1920 cartoon of the young domestic regretting her resignation could have been drawn in any of the previous twenty years.

Life continued along its habitual path with most of the original staff, though defections were coming too often. Publications such as *Cosmopolitan* and particularly the *New Yorker* were offering younger readers the stories, images, and photographs they craved.

Gibson drew cartoons for the next few years, but one has to question why? Why was the President of the company recycling much of his material from twenty-five years ago?

HER ONE REGRET AT LEAVING

Her One Regret
Life, February 12, 1920

Chapter 12 – Life Moves On

He evidently was not able to embrace the radical new art styles typified by the popular artist John Held Jr. By 1925 *Life* was publishing Held on its cover frequently, coinciding with Gibson's retreat from artistic production. Held's drawings personified the flapper era with gyrating characters dressed in sleek 1920s fashion. Bobbed hair, thin body lines and a two-dimension look – these images were anti-art to Gibson's Victorian styles. The caption on Held's February 18, 1926 cover for *Life* stated "Teaching Old Dogs New Tricks" was perhaps a metaphorical dagger to the old school's heart.

Except for a change of wardrobe, Gibson's scenarios and personalities as in *From Left to Right*, were from a previous era. They did not grab the younger set's attention or entice new subscribers.

Teaching Old Dogs New Tricks by John Held Jr.
Life, February 18, 1926

From Left to Right
♡ . . . ? . . . $

From Left to Right
An Old-School Gibson Cartoon
Life, February 9, 1922

Though still president of *Life*, Gibson soon retreated from daily appearances in the office. Essentially he retired to his 700 Acre Island off the Maine coast, delegating daily production and management to others. He also drew for other publications and even illustrated advertisements for companies such as Metropolitan Life. And once again, Gibson renewed his *Quixotic-like* challenge to become an accomplished oil painter.

Worse for *Life*, was the impending doom of the 1929 stock market crash and the resulting Great Depression. While the Wall Street panic marked the beginning of a failed economy, it had been faltering for years as banks across the country closed from a collapsing agriculture market and industrial speculation.

Having seen a similar economic disaster play out before, he remarked to biographer Downey with a bit of dark humor:

You can always tell when a panic is coming by when I start to paint.[4]

Gibson's pen seemed to draw its ink from his heart, this is seen throughout his fifty plus years of drawing. One of his last impacting images is evidence of the feeling and thought he put into a drawing, whether intentional or just natural.

Anno Domini — 1930 could be a Gibson Girl from a more prosperous time. His sketches over five decades always put women and children first, perhaps this was a deep-seated character trait developed from accepting responsibility for his mother and three sisters upon his father's death.

The soulful woman and innocent child reflected society and the country at a very sad time. The depression was taking a war-like toll on the people, business, and the nation.

The sadness was not just in the mother's face, but you feel it was in Gibson's heart as well.

Chapter 12 – Life Moves On

Anno Domini — 1930
Life, December 5, 1930

Anno Domini — 1930

• • •

C. D. Gibson's legacy was already well established as he once more continued his quest for painting excellence. Though he still had his apartment and studio in New York City, he enjoyed time on his island retreat working on the eighteen-room house he built in 1904, painting in his studio, and playing with his grandchildren and those of his brother Langdon who died in 1916.

Time Magazine paid tribute to him with its March 28, 1927 issue, including his picture on the cover. The accompanying story acknowledge that,

Gibson started operating in Manhattan in the late '80s . . . He took society for his province.

He grew rich, socially prominent, and accepted seriously the vogue he had created with polite mockery.

After he sold the last of his *Life* stock in 1932, the magazine continued to struggle until it was sold again in 1936, to *Time, Inc.* Henry Luce, chairman of *Time*, transformed it into his vision of a picture magazine, discarding the old ink drawings and humorous cartoons for photographs and stories of America and the world.

Gibson was now free to continue his often interrupted brush and color palette journey, already some his paintings were shown in small venues.

He was feted with dinners and inducted into virtually every society and institute that honored artists and humanitarians. Syracuse University conferred a degree as Doctor of Fine Arts[5] upon him. The Academy of Arts and Letters held a one-man show of his work in 1935, exhibiting not only eighty new paintings, but a separate gallery of pen-and-inks from the early days of *Life*.

Chapter 12 – Life Moves On

He continued a peaceful life with Irene and their family uninterrupted until he saw another great war engulf the world. Approaching seventy-five years old when Pearl Harbor was attacked, he engaged the war with haunting memories of the previous war and through the eyes of his son. Langhorne Gibson was born at an inopportune time, being of prime age to serve in the Navy during both The Great War and World War II.

• • •

There is no ideal time to die, some days are just worse than others. Two days before Christmas of 1944, Charles Dana Gibson died of heart failure while on his get-away island, most likely preparing for holiday cheer with his beloved family.

C. D. Gibson nourished a new genre of *social satire,* seducing the average person with everyday ironies and inequalities that he and the Gibson Girl so expertly revealed.

He experienced a magical transition period that was ushered in by the 20th century, and witnessed accompanying social changes such as child labor laws, women's right to vote, and anti-trust laws. Lucky for us, he recorded much of the era, as experienced by the Gibson Girl, so that we may enjoy his observations now just as his readers did then — and maybe learn some valuable lessons.

Epilogue

This book was conceived as a fun read and admiring survey of Charles Dana Gibson's unique humor, keen observations, and masterful artwork. Yet, as I followed his and the Gibson Girl's growth, and reflected on their clashes with heartless practices of the time, I saw frightening parallels with the state of America today. These included resurrection of some of the most grievous inequities that plagued yesteryear

Today we are witnessing persecution of others who are *not like me*, the intolerance of diverse religions and social practices, the lack of humility and compassion, the subtle imposition of economical and social class systems, and the use of fear, both real and imagined to justify these inequities. These unsavory behaviors were prevalent and seldom questioned at the turn of the 20th century, though the fictional Gibson Girl and throngs of real people were rising up to do the right thing.

Charles Dana Gibson and the Gibson Girl helped America embrace the 19th Amendment – and built respect for women's influence. It is worthwhile to repeat an earlier quote in this book as evidence – a portion of the platform from the Women's Democratic Club's in 1919:

> *". . . the right to cast her vote for such measures or candidates as are endorsed by her intellect and ratified by her conscience."*[1]

Moving forward one hundred years to today, it is not enough to simply vote. Concerned men and women, must make their positions clearly known and realize how their values can shape America, if not the world. As the centennial of the 19th Amendment approaches, we are again faced with misguided principles that were deemed unjust or even inhumane a century ago. Failure to stand up and be counted may cause our children and grandchildren to fight these same battles over and over.

Along the way, the Gibson Girl helped empower women, the young, old, and disadvantaged by bringing their plight to the attention of her reader's conscience. It would be inaccurate to imply she was the major or only force in action. There were legions of women performing in the role of *boots on the ground*. They picketed the White House, organized rallies, held town meetings, marched in parades, and educated followers and doubters alike. The Gibson Girl was a supporting face of progress. For three decades, her weekly appearances in front of millions of readers reinforced the modern message in-between the suffragists' organized events.

Just as the Gibson Girl reached many people, today's informed citizens choose from a variety of print, broadcast, and online sources. Indeed, each individual also has their own means to communicate with thousands if not millions through social media apps. This gives everyone the opportunity to be an influential Gibson Girl – though wielding this power one should remember the oft-quoted *"With great power comes great responsibility"*.

The goal of this book is to remind the reader that we have seen the results of fear and intolerance before. Yet once again, history is attempting to repeat itself. Hopefully, *Lessons from the Gibson Girl* will inspire you to stand up for decency, fairness, and equality.

• • •

Lessons From The Gibson Girl

Bibliography

Books by C. D. Gibson

The large (17.5" x 11.5") table books are compilations of many cartoons drawn in the year previous to publication, plus additional sketches. Out of print, they can be found on popular auction sites and in many libraries.

Gibson, Charles Dana. *Drawings*. New York: R. H. Russell, 1894.

— *Pictures of People*. New York: R. H. Russell, 1896.

— *London as Seen by Charles Dana Gibson*. New York: R. H. Russell, 1897.

— *Sketches and Cartoons*. New York: R. H. Russell, 1898.

— *The Education of Mr. Pipp*. New York: R. H. Russell, 1899.

— *Americans*. New York: R. H. Russell, 1900.

— *A Widow and Her Friends*. New York: R. H. Russell, 1901.

— *The Social Ladder*. New York: R. H. Russell, 1902.

— *The Weaker Sex*. New York: Charles Scribner's Sons, 1903.

— *Every Day People*. New York: Charles Scribner's Sons, 1904.

— *Our Neighbors*, New York: Charles Scribner's Sons, 1905.

General

Biographical books for those interested in Gibson, Richard Harding Davis, and others. Most are out of print, though they can be found on used book websites and online auctions, or available in libraries. The two books by Fairfax Downey are exceptional resources.

Downey, Fairfax. *Portrait of an Era - As Drawn by C. D. Gibson*. New York: Charles Scribner's Sons, 1936.

Knowlton, Josephine Gibson. *Longfield: The House on the Neck*. Providence: Oxford Press, 1956.

Downey, Fairfax. *Richard Harding Davis - His day*. New York: Charles Scribner's Sons, 1933.

Lidbow, Arthur. *The Reporter Who Would Be King*. New York: Charles Scribner's Sons, 1992.

Chambers, Robert W. *The Common Law*. New York: Grosset & Dunlap, 1911.

Magruder, Julia. *The Princess Sonia*. New York: The Century Co., 1895.

Davis, Richard Harding. *Soldiers of Fortune*. New York: Charles Scribner's Sons, 1914.

Davis, Charles Belmont. *Adventures and Letters of Richard Harding Davis*. New York: Charles Scribner's Sons, 1918.

Rawls, Walton. *Wake Up, America! World War I and the American Poster*. New York: Abbeville Press, 1988.

Notes

Introduction - Hooked on Gibson
1. Frederick W. Morton, "Charles Dana Gibson Illustrator", *Brush and Pencil*, February 1901.

Chapter 1 - Imagination and Wit
1. Fairfax Downey, *Portrait of an Era, As Drawn by C. D. Gibson* (New York: Charles Scribner's Sons, 1936) 5.

Chapter 2 - Becoming the Artist
1. Fairfax Downey, *Portrait of an Era, As Drawn by C. D. Gibson* (New York: Charles Scribner's Sons, 1936) 41.
2. "The Historic Elephant and Donkey", *New York Times*, August 2, 1908.
3. *Thomas Nast Biography*, Ohio State University Web Site, http://cartoons.osu.edu/digital_albums/thomasnast/bio.htm, 24 December 2015.
4. Fairfax Downey, *Portrait of an Era, As Drawn by C. D. Gibson* (New York: Charles Scribner's Sons, 1936) 84.
5. Josephine Gibson Knowlton, *Longfield: The House on the Neck* (Providence R.I., Oxford Press, 1956) 293.
6. John Ames Mitchell, Wikipedia, https://en.wikipedia.org/wiki/John_Ames_Mitchell, accessed Feb 22, 2016.
7. J.A. Mitchell, *That First Affair and Other Sketches* (New York: Charles Scribner's Sons, 1896).
8. Fairfax Downey, *Portrait of an Era, As Drawn by C. D. Gibson*, (New York: Charles Scribner's Sons, 1936) 88.
9. Fred R. Barnard, "One Look is Worth a Thousand Words", *Printer's Ink*, December 8, 1921.

Chapter 3 - American Society
1. National American Woman Suffrage Association, Wikipedia, https://en.wikipedia.org/wiki/National_American_Woman_Suffrage_Association, accessed Feb 6, 2016.
2. *Fore (golf)*, Wikipedia, www.en.wikipedia.org/wiki/Fore_(golf), accessed July 11, 2015.
3. *Wheels of Change: The Bicycle and Women's Rights*, Sarah Nipper, MS Magazine Blog, http://msmagazine.com/blog/2014/05/07/wheels-of-change-the-bicycle-and-womens-rights/, accessed Jan 12, 2016. Or *What Shall the New Woman Wear, Skirts or Bloomers*,Los Angeles Herald, Los Angeles September 15, 1895, 14.
4. Dominion Medical Journal, Toronto, July 1898, p. 28 www.en.wikipedia.org/wiki/Fore_(golf), accessed July 11, 2015.
5. J. Cardinal Gibbons, "The Restless Woman", *Ladies Home Journal*, January 1902.
6. "Champion Of Her Sex: Miss Susan B. Anthony", *The New York World*, February 2, 1896.
7. Burning Tree Club, oobgolf.com, www.oobgolf.com, http://www.oobgolf.com/courses/course/7092/Burning_Tree_Club.html accessed July 18, 2015.
8. Burning Tree Club, Wikipedia, https://en.wikipedia.org/wiki/Burning_Tree_Club, accessed April 15, 1916
9. Steve Rushin, "Mass Hysteria", *Sports Illustrated*, September 28, 2015.
10. "Will Visit Sir Thomas Lipton", *The Brooklyn Daily Eagle*, January 15, 1904.

11. "Miss Gibson Not To Marry", *The New York Times*, May 13, 1912.

12. The Fresh Air Fund, http://www.freshair.org/learn-about-us, accessed March 30, 1916.

13. Frederick W. Morton. "Charles Dana Gibson Illustrator", *Brush and Pencil*, February 1901.

14. Robert Bridges, "Charles Dana Gibson, An Appreciation", *Collier's*, October 15, 1904.

Chapter 4 - The Gibson Girl

1. Fairfax Downey, *Portrait of an Era as Drawn by C. D Gibson* (New York: Charles Scribner's Sons, 1933).

2. Ibid. p. 17.

3. Ibid. p. 20.

4. Josephine Gibson Knowlton, *Longfield: The House on the Neck* (Providence: Oxford Press, 1956) 243.

5. "Photo-Mechanical Processes", *New York Times*, November 16, 1890.

6. Oscar Wilde, "The Decay of Lying", Essay, 1889.

7. Bernard Saw, *Three Plays for Puritans* (Chicago & New York: Herbert S. Stone, 1901) xviii.

8. Edward Marshall, "The Gibson Girl Analyzed by Her Originator", *New York Times*, November 20, 1910.

9. "A White City Model, Woman Who Posed for the Statue of the Republics", *Chicago Daily Tribune*, December 29, 1894.

10. *Brooklyn Daily Eagle*, Oct 14, 1894.

11. Ibid, p. 13.

12. "The American Artist", *The Courier*, December 19, 1894.

13. Scarbrough, Emily, ""Fine Dignity, Picturersque Beauty, and Serious Purpose": The Reorientation of Suffrage Media in the Twentieth Century (2015) Masters Theses. Paper 2033, http://thekeep.eiu.edu/theses/2033.

14. Mary Walton, *A Woman's Crusade, Alice Paul And The Battle For The Ballot* (New York: Palgrave Macmillian, 2010) 8.

15. Jean H. Baker, Sisters, *The Lives of America's Suffragists* (New York, Hill and Wang, 2005) 192.

Chapter 5 – The Gibson Man

1. Josephine Gibson Knowlton, *Longfield: The House on the Neck* (Providence: Oxford Press, 1956) 243.

2. Fairfax Downey, *Richard Harding Davis, His Day* (New York: Charles Scribner's Sons, 1933) 3.

3. Peter Griffin, *Along with Youth: Hemingway, the Early Years* (New York: Oxford University Press, 1983) 39.

4. Charles Belmont Davis, *Adventures and Letters of Richard Harding Davis* (New York: Charles Scribner's Sons, 1918) 16.

5. Charles Belmont Davis, *Adventures and Letters of Richard Harding Davis* (New York: Charles Scribner's Sons, 1918) 57.

6. Richard Harding Davis, *The First Shot of the War*, Scribner's, July 1898.

7. Richard Harding Davis, *The Battle of San Juan*, Scribner's, October 1898.

8. Richard Harding Davis, *Three Gringos in Venezuela* (New York: Harper & Brothers Publishers, 1896).

Chapter 6 – Rise to Fame

1. AdvertisingAge, Nast, Conde (1873-1942), accessed November 20, 2015, http://adage.com/article/adage-encyclopedia/nast-conde-1873-1942/98791/.
2. *Collier's Weekly*, February 7, 1903.
3. Measuring Worth, accessed November 20, 2015, http://www.measuringworth.com/uscompare/relativevalue.php.
4. "Gibson's Abandonment Of The Pen For The Brush", *Current Literature*, December 1905.
5. "Disney Threw Out George Lucas' Episode VII ", slashfilm.com http://www.slashfilm.com/george-lucas-star-wars-episode-vii/, accessed November 23, 2015. Also *Vanity Fair* June 2015.
6. Arthur Lubow, *The Reporter Who Would Be King* (New York: Charles Scribner's Sons, 1992) 67.
7. Melissa R. Pompili, *Transatlantic Intimacies: The Homoerotic Affect Worlds of Nineteenth-Century Print Culture* (MA thesis, Eastern Michigan University, 2013). http://commons.emich.edu/theses/489/, accessed November 23, 2015.
8. "Gibson's Abandonment Of The Pen For The Brush", Current Literature, December 1905.

Chapter 8 – A Real Gibson Girl

1. Irene Langhorne, Encyclopedia Virginia, http://www.encyclopediavirginia.org/Gibson_Irene_Langhorne_1873-1956, accessed Dec. 1, 2015.
2. Chiswell Langhorne, Wikepedia, https://en.wikipedia.org/wiki/Chiswell_Langhorne, accessed Dec. 1, 2015.
3. Fairfax Downey, *Portrait of an Era, As Drawn by C. D. Gibson* (New York: Charles Scribner's Sons, 1936) 215-218.
4. Ibid., 224.
5. "Wedding Bells in Richmond", *Philadelphia Times*, November 8, 1895, 1.
6. "A Notable Richmond Wedding", *Roanoke Times*, November 8,1895, 1.
7. Fairfax Downey, *Portrait of an Era, As Drawn by C. D. Gibson* (New York: Charles Scribner's Sons, 1936) 232.
8. Ibid., 230.
9. "Gibson Girls' Creator and American Girl Types", *The New York Times*, April 30, 1905.
10. *The New York Charities Directory*, Charity Organization Society, New York, 1920.
11. "Women Form Organization to Aid Democrats", *New York Tribune*, December 26, 1919.

Chapter 9 – Pursuing a Dream

1. William Griffith, "Gibson Girls' Creator and American Girl Types", *New York Times*, April 30, 1905.
2. "C. D. Gibson Sails", *New York Times*, December 1, 1905, p. 9.
3. Ibid.
4. *New York Times*, December 2, 1905.

Chapter 10 – Noir et Blanc

1. "C. D. Gibson Returns to Black and White", *The New York Times*, November 12, 1908.

2. Fairfax Downey, *Portrait of an Era, As Drawn by C. D. Gibson* (New York: Charles Scribner's Sons, 1936) 305.

3. Robert W. Chambers, *The Common Law* (New York: Grosset & Dunlap, 1911).

4. Fairfax Downey, *Portrait of an Era, As Drawn by C. D. Gibson* (New York: Charles Scribner's Sons, 1936) 306.

5. Fairfax Downey, *Portrait of an Era, As Drawn by C. D. Gibson* (New York: Charles Scribner's Sons, 1936) 310; and *Cosmopolitan*, April, 1912.

Chapter 11 – Gibson Girl Goes to War

1. National Archives, *The Zimmermann Telegram*, https://www.archives.gov/education/lessons/zimmermann/#documents.

2. Fairfax Downey, *Portrait of an Era as Drawn by C. D Gibson* (New York: Charles Scribner's Sons, 1933) 269.

3 Walton Rawls, *Wake Up, America!, World War I and The American Poster* (New York: Abeville Press, 1988) 149.

4. "C. D. Gibson's Committee for Patriotic Posters", *The New York Times Magazine,* January 20, 1918.

5 Walton Rawls, *Wake Up, America!, World War I and The American Poster* (New York: Abeville Press, 1988) 150.

6. "C. D. Gibson's Committee for Patriotic Posters", *The New York Times Magazine,* January 20, 1918.

7. Fairfax Downey, *Portrait of an Era as Drawn by C. D Gibson* (New York: Charles Scribner's Sons, 1933) 326.

8. Walton Rawls, *Wake Up, America!, World War I and The American Poster* (New York: Abeville Press, 1988) 167.

9. Ibid. 168.

Chapter 12 – Life Moves On

1. Fairfax Downey, *Portrait of an Era as Drawn by C. D Gibson* (New York: Charles Scribner's Sons, 1933) 348.

2. Ibid. 348.

2. Ibid. 355.

4. Ibid. 360

5. Ibid. 368

Epilogue

1. "Women Form Organization to Aid Democrats", *New York Tribune*, December 26, 1919.

Index

19th Amendment 46, 216

A

Adams, Maude 81
All American Woman 14
American Girl 71
Angel of Death 75
Anthony, Susan B. 53
Archduke Ferdinand 240
Art Students League 25, 26
Atelier Julien 39
Augusta National Golf Club 53
Austro-Hungarian 240

B

Balestier, Wolcott 33
Barrymore, Ethel , 81
Benedict, Helen 210
Bicycles 48
Bloomers 49
Burning Tree Golf Club 53

C

Cardinal Gibbons 51
Chambers, Robert W. 25, 232
Christy, Howard Chandler 222
Clark, Minnie 74
Collier's Contract 98
Creel, George 247
Cupid 112

D

Davis, Charles Belmont 92
Davis, Richard Harding 90, 94, 110, 103, , 95
DeKay, James 90, 95
Doonesbury 30
Downey, Fairfax 65, 232

E

Erotica 102

F

Fawcett, Farrah 70
First Affair, The 36
Flagg, James Montgomery 251
Franklin, Benjamin 28
French, Daniel 75

G

Gibson, Charley 20, 39
Gibson, Josephine 59
Gibson, Langdon 40, 88, 95
Gibson, Langhorne 248
Giibson, Josephine Elizabeth 66
Gilded Age 43
Golf 47, 53
Great War, The 24, 237

H

Harper's 28
Hawthorne, Rev T. D. 49
Hemingway, Eernest 92

Index

I
Ipswich Hosiery 27

J
Join or Die 28
Judge 30

L
Langhorne, Chiswell 206
Langhorne, Irene 84, 205, 208, 215, 218
Lefebvre, Jules Joseph 39
Lipton, Sir Thomas 59
Little Susanne 75
Lovett, Josephine DeWolf 66

M
Magruder, Julia 104
Master's Tournament 53
Maurier, George du 31, 38
Miller, Andrew 34
Mitchell, John A. 32, 34, 35, 62, 240, 241

N
Nast, Thomas 29
Nesbit, Evelyn 79

P
Perard, Victor 225
Pompili, Melissa R. 106
Princess Sonia 105, 106
Progressive Era 44
P. T. Barnum 21
Punch 30

R
Remington, Fredric 25
Rice, Conoleezza 53
Rometty, Ginni 53
Roosevelt, Alice 79
Roosevelt, Teddy 94
Rough Riders 94
Russell, Robert H. 52, 205, 210

S
San Juan Hill 72
Santa Claus 29
Scribner's 28
Society of Illustrators 247
Spanish American War 93
Spears, Britney 70
Suffrage 45

T
Tid-Bits 30, 32, 33, 35
Trudeau, Garry 30

W
Wilde, Oscar 70

Books by Gary W. Clark

Historical

Cruel Irony
Triumphs and Tragedies of a Modern Woman.

FUBAR 2.0
A Soldier's Insight into Military Chaos.

Photography

Photo Restoration
A Step-by-Step Guide for Repairing Photographs with Photoshop Elements.

20th Century Photographs
A Guide to Identifying and Dating Photographs from 1900 to 1950.

19th Century Card Photos
A Step-by-Step Guide to Identifying and Dating Cartes de Visite and Cabinet Cards.

Cased Images and Tintypes
A Guide to Identifying and Dating Daguerreotypes, Ambrotypes, and Tintypes.

Real Photo Postcards
A Guide to Identifying and Dating Real Photo Postcards of the 20th Century.

Archive Photography
How to Photograph Oversize Photos, Curled documents, and Heirloom Treasures.

Gravestone Photography and Documentation
Document Ancestor Graves with Photographs and Location Data.

Slides and Negatives
Digitize and Protect Your Vintage Film.

All books are available from Amazon.com.

Visit the author's Amazon page:
  http://www.amazon.com/author/Gary-Clark

Email: gary@garywclark.com
Web: www.garywclark.com

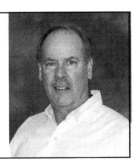

Made in the USA
Lexington, KY
08 August 2017